Alan St. Aubyn

A tragic Honeymoon

Vol. I

Alan St. Aubyn

A tragic Honeymoon
Vol. I

ISBN/EAN: 9783337050931

Printed in Europe, USA, Canada, Australia, Japan

Cover: Foto ©ninafisch / pixelio.de

More available books at **www.hansebooks.com**

A TRAGIC HONEYMOON.

A Novel.

BY

ALAN ST. AUBYN,

AUTHOR OF
"A FELLOW OF TRINITY,"
"THE OLD MAID'S SWEETHEART," "THE JUNIOR DEAN,"
ETC., ETC.

IN TWO VOLUMES.

VOL. I.

LONDON:
F. V. WHITE & Co.,
14, BEDFORD STREET, STRAND, W.C.
1894.

PRINTED BY
KELLY AND CO. LIMITED, 182, 183 AND 184, HIGH HOLBORN, W.C.
AND MIDDLE MILL, KINGSTON-ON-THAMES.

CONTENTS.

CHAP.		PAGE
I.—The Curate of St. Radegund's	. .	1
II.—Cherry Garden	. . . . .	26
III.—Nearer and Nearer	. . . .	55
IV.—Ladylift	. . . . .	72
V.—Paradise	. . . . .	90
VI.—Nancy's Lovers	. . . .	114
VII.—"That Forward Minx!"	. . .	135
VIII.—"Tum-tum-te-tumty"	. . .	153
IX.—"Douglas, Douglas, Tender and True"		169
X.—Sarah Strong	. . . .	185
XI.—"A Little Rift Within the Lute"	.	200
XII.—In the Rain	. . . .	217

A TRAGIC HONEYMOON.

A TRAGIC HONEYMOON.

CHAPTER I.

THE CURATE OF ST. RADEGUND'S.

"What eyes, like thine, have waken'd hopes?"

It was whispered in Stoke Edith — whispered softly across the tea tables — that the curate of St. Radegund's was in love with Nancy Coulcher. Everybody was sorry for him; the men smiled and shook their heads knowingly, as if they could tell if they would, what would be the poor fellow's fate, and the women sighed. Their sorrow for the gentle-natured curate who had recently come among them, and had won all their tender hearts, was genuine, quite genuine, and they all agreed that he deserved a better fate.

Nancy Coulcher was not a favourite with the mothers and daughters of Stoke Edith. The ladies of Stoke did not admire her so much as the gentlemen did, perhaps if they had, she would not have been immensely gratified. She preferred the admiration of men; she generally got quite as much admiration as she desired, which is saying a great deal.

She was a man's beauty, not a woman's beauty. There was not a woman in Stoke Edith who could understand what the men could find to rave about in her.

They raved nevertheless. Perhaps a little beauty of a certain sort — not a very refined sort—went a great way with them. Besides, Nancy Coulcher was the fashion at the time. Men are like sheep, they are content to follow where others lead.

She had a delightful way with her lovers, a frank *camaraderie* that took immensely, and set them all at their ease. The women called it by another name, an old-fashioned name—they did not mince matters—they called it forwardness.

The old women of Stoke were behind the time: girls behaved better, no doubt, when they were young—there was not so much freedom and license, and there was no *camaraderie*. Her worst enemies could not call Nancy a flirt—a flirt is a creature of wiles and stratagems, full of airs and graces, and laying traps for men. Nancy had no need to lay traps; her victims crowded round her unsought—she had no need to resort to stratagem. She received them all with her ready smiles, and an engaging frankness of manner that was very sweet and taking, but utterly meaningless.

Perhaps this was the secret of her success. Masculine vanity had a good deal to do with it. Every one of Nancy

Coulcher's adorers believed that he was the favoured object of her young affections. Her ready smiles didn't mean much, but they conveyed a good deal, and were very transferable. She had a manner too, that took with men, a sweet artless manner of tender appealing helplessness, of advice-seeking and aid-demanding that went straight to the hearts of her dupes and made them more her slaves than ever. When our story opens she was the standing toast of Stoke Edith; she was brighter, prettier, and more daring than any other girl in the place—and she was not troubled with scruples. She pleased herself. Why shouldn't a girl please herself?—is it not the order of the day?

Nancy Coulcher had so many lovers, she might have spared the curate of St. Radegund's. A poor curate with a wretched stipend of one hundred and fifty pounds a year was not much of a conquest.

A heart more or less made so little difference to her.

It would have been kinder to have spared him—kinder and wiser. It would have been more womanly to have been content with her conquests, and let the foolish curate go.

Nancy was not made on noble lines; she was only a shallow, frivolous thing who had the gift of beauty. An accident—a happy accident—the droop of an eyelid, the curve of a rounded cheek, thin, scarlet lips, that were always breaking into laughter, lovely little sharp white teeth, a ready knack of blushing—and sweet eyes.

A woman's eyes ought to have a soul behind them, but Nancy Coulcher's blue eyes were shallow, like her nature. Empty and shallow, with a sweet, shy, pathetic droop of the long-fringed eyelids that veiled their emptiness.

Perhaps this was where the subtle charm

came in. Women could never be got to see it, but men went down before it.

The curate of Stoke Edith went down with the rest. He didn't go down at once, he resisted longer than the rest—he was more exercised in spiritual warfare, in wrestling with the old Adam. But he went down at last, and his fall was all the harder from having held out so long.

Douglas Craik had been in Holy Orders three years when he came to Stoke Edith; he had been working all that time in a dreadful London slum. He had gone through as much in those three years as most men go through in a lifetime. He had seen more suffering and sin, and poverty and misfortune and sorrow—real sorrow— than most men. The sad sights he had seen, and the sadder knowledge of the realities of life that had come to him had touched him, as they could not fail to touch a highly-strung sympathetic nature, and deepened the earnestness, the intense earnestness of his character. He could do nothing by halves, realizing as he did the awful responsibilities of this present life, and the tremendous outlook of the future.

He threw himself into his work, soul and body. He had a great deal of the former, and little, very little of the latter—he never spared himself, and the consequence was that at the end of three years' work in a crowded London parish he was utterly and completely broken down—a mere wreck of his former self, and had to be sent into the country for a change.

He would never be fit for London work again, the eminent physician said, who pronounced his life sentence. He would never be fit for anything but light duty in a healthy country parish. The duty at Stoke Edith was light, and the air was fine, particularly fine. It brought roses into the cheeks of the girls, and of the boys too, as it happened to be the seat of a large public school with three or four hundred boys.

There was not much else at Stoke Edith but the grammar school, and the salubrious air, but it was quite enough to bring people from all parts of England to settle in the neighbourhood. It brought an unusual number of widows. Perhaps because the school was cheap, and widows with boys to educate are seldom overburdened with wealth.

Among the widows came Mrs. Coulcher and her boys, and three grown-up daughters, from a village in Cornwall of which her husband had been rector. The girls were all grown up when she came to Stoke Edith, but the boys were still quite young. There were three of them now at the grammar school, and one away at the University. The eldest, Geoff, had won a scholarship, or he would not have been able to go up to Cambridge. It was only a sixty-pound scholarship from the school, and his mother had to make up the difference. He had been "up" a year already, and the "difference" and the college bills that came in at the end of the year had threatened to swallow up her slender income.

It had been little enough to begin with, to bring up seven children upon, but carefully eked out, it had served, like the widow's cruse, to meet the humble demands upon it. Now it seemed that Geoff was going to take it all; that there would be nothing left for the rest. But this was not all; troubles seldom come alone. A colonial bank in which the principal part of Mrs. Coulcher's small fortune was invested had stopped payment, and her dividends had suddenly ceased.

. This financial crisis had not arisen in the Coulcher establishment until some months after Douglas Craik came to Stoke Edith. Looking across the pews of St. Radegund's one April night when he gave out the hymns, and all the time he was preaching his little earnest sermon, he could have seen the cloud resting on the widow's worn face, as she sat among her boys under the south window. He would certainly have seen it and recognised it had he looked her way—for who should be more quick to note the flag of distress than he? He knew the lines of sorrow, and suffering, and care so well; he had mastered all the touches of those hard masters; he recognised them in a moment, but he had only eyes for one face in that seat beneath the "south window," the face of Mrs. Coulcher's youngest daughter.

Douglas Craik reading the beautiful downcast face between the lines of his sermon, saw that there was something wrong. There was a pathetic droop of the red under lip that he had not observed before, and the sweet eyes were downcast. Once or twice he thought Nancy Coulcher was going to cry. He would have given the world to have shut up his sermon-case and got down from the pulpit, and gone over to the pew beneath the great window and comforted her, but he sighed, and restrained himself, and went on with his sermon. He met Lucy Coulcher, the second girl, the next day, and enquired anxiously after her sister.

Lucy Coulcher was a common-place sort of a girl, that is, she was exactly like a thousand, like a hundred thousand, other girls. There was nothing distinctive about her. She was not the least like her beautiful sister. She hadn't either the beauty or the airs or graces of Nancy, there was no pensive droop of her very common-place eyelids over her very common-place eyes. They were clear, honest eyes, and they looked straight out at you behind her glasses — Lucy wore glasses — she had not Nancy's fascinating way of looking at people — masculine people; her features were blunt, and her figure short and plump. She was always going about the parish, visiting and leaving tracts, and reading to bedridden old men and women.

She was generally known in Stoke Edith as "the good Miss Coulcher," and Augusta, the elder sister, enjoyed the distinction of "the clever Miss Coulcher."

Lucy Coulcher blushed when she saw the Curate coming across the road to speak to her on that April morning. He was a pale, slim young man, with a fine, clear-cut face, rather a delicate, refined face, and the colour mounted up into it as he crossed the road to ask Lucy after her sister. She saw the unwonted colour in the Curate's face, and she blushed too.

It was a perfect Spring morning with the

blue April sky above, and all the world breaking into blossom at her feet. The new blood of the Spring was in everything, the flowers were crowding out in the hedges, and the lilac was nodding over the garden wall as Lucy stopped beneath it to shake hands with the Curate.

Perhaps this had something to do with her blushing. The new blood of the Spring was tingling in her veins, in her finger tips as well as in the lilac buds overhead, and it mounted up into her plain, freckled face when she saw Douglas Craik hurrying up the street towards her. Lucy had an absurd habit of blushing, but she had a kindly manner which took immensely with all the old women in the parish.

"Poor old Sarah Strong is no better this morning," he said, speaking hurriedly to hide his ridiculous confusion. "I have just come from her. She was too ill to bear any reading—perhaps——"

He had no need to finish the sentence. Lucy knew exactly what he was going to say.

"Of course I'll go to her," she said readily. "If she cannot bear any reading, I can sit with her. She is always glad of anyone to sit with her. It must be dreadfully lonely for her, being left so many, many hours alone."

"Yes," said the curate absently, but he was not thinking of Sarah Strong. "I—I thought your sister was not looking very well last night. I hope she is better this morning."

"Oh, Augusta had the toothache; she always looks glum when she has the toothache; she is better this morning."

Then the curate had to explain that it was not the eldest Miss Coulcher he was enquiring for. He had not noticed that poor Augusta had a swollen face.

"Nancy's quite well, thank you," Lucy

said, rather tartly. She had no patience with men always enquiring after Nancy. "I daresay she was looking rather glum. She's going to give lessons on the violin at Miss Mallet's this term; she won't have so much time for tennis, and I am going to take an ambulance class, and teach German. We've all got to do something to help mother. You've heard of mother's losses. There are the three boys to educate, and Geoff at college; we couldn't all stay at home doing nothing."

The curate murmured something idiotic to the effect that it was very praiseworthy of three stalwart girls to do something to help a poor broken-down parent. He thought Lucy was quite right to "go out," but Nancy—his cheeks paled at the thought of Nancy Coulcher going out into the world to earn her living.

Lucy's grey eyes read his thoughts like an open book. She had no patience with him. She turned up her little blunt *retroussé* nose and went on her way raging inwardly.

"They are all exactly alike," she said impatiently. "I never thought *he* would be such a fool as the rest!"

Lucy was as good as her word. She went to see Sarah Strong at once. She hadn't any tracts with her this morning, or her Bible tucked under her arm, and she had not intended to do any visiting. She had started early to do some shopping. Nature had already, with a great deal of rustling and bustling, unpacked her fresh Spring clothing, and discarded her shabby old brown winter wraps. The ground was strewn with the worn-out old husks that the dear little green buds overhead had thrown off, and here was Lucy still in her dowdy winter frock.

She sighed and put the bits of print she was going to match into her pocket, and turned away from the High Street with its dazzling shops into a quarter where the humbler people dwelt.

It was an unsavoury quarter; it was full of small, poor houses huddled together, and the sanitation was not all that could be desired. It was a blot upon Stoke Edith. This little neglected slum was known as "Paradise," not in irony, oh, dear no! It had once been a delightful suburb of the old, old town, and its thatched cottages and dear little gardens, with the woodbine growing over the porch, and the orchards blossoming behind, and the sweet green country spreading around it had won for it this distinguished appellation.

It was Paradise still, though the gardens had disappeared, and the orchards bloomed no longer, and the houses had crowded closer together, blotting out the sweet green country. Love was still there. Love ready to bear, and strong to save. Love in all its varied forms; mother-love, child-love, the love of sweethearts and wives. Wherever men, women, and little children are, whatever else there is, there is always love. Love is happiness, love is life, love is something deeper than happiness, and more enduring than life.

What more is wanted to make Paradise?

Into this Paradise Lucy Coulcher entered, and found her way up a narrow staircase into a darkened room, where there was an old woman slowly dying of—well, of nothing particular, of the common disease of the poor; old age, rheumatism, poverty. It was a wonder she had lived so long. She was so old; she had suffered from rheumatism for years; ever since Lucy was born, she could not turn in bed without groaning; she could not lie in one position for any length of time—and she was miserably poor. There was nothing for poor old Sarah Strong to live for, but she went on living. She was tough and long-lived, and unless something quite unexpected came upon her, she might go on groaning for some time to come.

Lucy Coulcher entered the room without knocking; she would have had a long time to wait for an anwer.

The room was dark and close on this sweet spring morning; it had been shut up all night; it had been shut up for days and days, the windows had not been opened for months, and nobody had thought of drawing the blinds up to let in the warm April sunshine.

Lucy went up to the bed and said a few words to the old woman in her kind, soft voice, and then she drew up the blind, and the sunshine streamed into the room and across the bed. The old woman put up her feeble hands to keep out the light.

"Pull it down, dearie," she moaned, "pull it down, I can't abear it!"

"I'm sure it will do you good, Sarah; the sunshine does everything good. You will be able to bear it presently."

"I can't abear it," the old woman said fretfully. "I've done with it, like I've done with most things. I've been mortal bad since you were here last. I never thought to have seen the light o' the sun again. Pull it down, dearie, pull it down!"

There was nothing to be done but to pull the blind down, and the bare chilly room was again in darkness.

"Is there anything I can do for you, Sarah?" Lucy asked softly, "shall I read to you?"

"No, dearie, I can't abear reading, I'm past most things."

"You could bear a psalm, a few words, a text, I'm sure, Sarah?"

"I can't bear naught. I've done wi' preachin' an' prayin' an' readin'. I've hearkened to 'em all my life, an' I'm none the better for 'em now."

"If you can't bear reading, perhaps you'd like me to sit with you for a little time," Lucy said with a sigh; it was so difficult to find anything to say to this cantankerous old woman. "I'm sure you must get very tired lying here alone so many hours."

"I get dreadful tired an' sick, an' lonesome, an' the pain is that bad sometimes I pray to be took. I dunno what I be kep' lying here for, day after day, an' night after night, an' getting no rest for the pain."

"The Lord knows," Lucy said softly. She did not venture to suggest that there was a reason for the poor old worn-out body to be kept groaning here on a bed of pain. She did not dare to say that perhaps there was a need-be for this discipline of suffering.

"Ay, he knows, I s'pose!" the old woman said fretfully, "unless he's a-forgotten me. "I'm most tired of askin' him to take the pain away. I've gone on askin' an' askin', an' its worse than ever. Oh! Oh!"

She was trying to move in the bed, and the movement brought on the pain, which was seldom absent for more than a few minutes together. She was propped up in the bed with pillows, and her feeble groping hands lay outside on the coverlet. They were thin, brown, shrivelled hands, and her nails were long like a bird's claws, and the poor worn old face was a net-work of wrinkles.

Lucy smoothed her pillows, and drew back the straggling locks of her scanty grey hair, and drew her old ragged shawl about her.

"Have you asked Him for patience?" Lucy said softly as she was bending over her. "Patience to bear the pain and the suffering He has thought fit to lay upon you?"

"Patience!" the old woman repeated with a sniff. "You'd talk of patience if you lay here a-groanin' day after day, an' not a wink of sleep o' nights for the pain! Patience! My patience's most a-weared out; what wi' the pain, and what wi' the tiredness, an' lying here alone in the dark, hour after hour—an' never seein' a human face, nor feelin' the touch of a human hand. It's the only comfort I've got in life to feel the touch of a hand now an' then. If I'd got that to cling to, I could do wi'out patience."

It was no use to argue with the old woman. Not a single gleam of light would penetrate the darkness of her soul. No reading or prayers would pierce the gathering gloom.

It seemed, as the Curate had said, quite

a hopeless case; but Lucy was not to be daunted.

"I'm not in a hurry this morning, Sarah," she said, sitting down in a chair beside the bed, and taking one of the feeble hands on the coverlet in hers. "I will sit with you for an hour if you like, and perhaps you can get a little sleep. if I hold your hand. Don't be afraid of going to sleep, I won't go away."

The feeble clinging fingers closed round Lucy's soft warm hand; she could not have taken it away if she would, and the old woman lay muttering to herself:

"It's the feel of the flesh does me good, dearie, it's something to cling to."

How long Lucy sat there, she could not tell. The air of the darkened room was stifling and oppressive; she would have given anything to have pulled up the blind an inch that a ray of sunlight might have entered, but she did not dare to stir from her place.

Sarah Strong had fallen asleep with Lucy's hand in hers. She could not have disengaged it if she would; the long lean fingers, more like the talons of a bird than anything human, had twined themselves around it, and held it in a grip of iron. It was like the clutch of a drowning wretch clinging for bare life.

Lucy sat by the old woman's side till she awoke, listening to the sounds of life in the court outside, the women's voices, and the children at play, and the monotonous ticking of a clock in the room below, with a dreadful, dreadful doubt gnawing at her heart, as if the evil spirit that possessed Sarah Strong had passed from the worn-out body on the bed, in that long hand clasp, into her.

Perhaps it had.

CHAPTER II.

CHERRY GARDEN.

> "You know so ill to deal with time,
> You needs must play such pranks as these."

CHERRY GARDEN, as the street where Mrs. Coulcher lived was called, took its name from an old cherry orchard, that used to flourish on the outskirts of the town years and years ago, before the widow had found out the advantages of the grammar school.

The town had been growing ever since they had made the discovery, and rows of neat semi-detached villas, with dreadful uniformity, had sprung up on every side. They had crept over the green fields, and down the meadows to the river's bank, and up the hill sides. They had invaded the old cherry orchard, and bit by bit it had been built over. There was nothing left of it now but the name, and that had lost its original savour; it was a garden now, not an orchard, "Cherry Garden." Orchards are so plebeian; nobody lives in orchards now, they smack of the damp moist earth; an odour of freshness and greenness hangs about them, a suggestion of cool rain, of the damp fragrance of the country, of green grass and things growing and blossoming, of rushing winds and the swaying of branches, and the patter of rain drops on the leaves.

Nobody would ever think of living in an orchard.

Mrs. Coulcher lived in the corner house of Cherry Garden, which had the advantage over the rest of the row, that it looked both ways. This was sometimes a convenience; visitors could be seen approaching from opposite directions, and if they were at all likely to clash, arrangements could be made accordingly.

Nancy Coulcher, standing at the big bay window that commanded the double view, saw the curate of St. Radegund coming up the street, and another gentleman approaching from an opposite direction.

They were both coming towards Cherry Garden, and they were both coming to call.

It was Mrs. Coulcher's "At Home" day, and there were already two or three people in the room, and Augusta and her mother were talking to them.

Mrs. Coulcher was trying to listen to the platitudes of some tiresome callers, but her mind was far away. She was worrying and wearying about those debts of Geoffrey's, and the bank shares that had stopped paying dividends, and she was wondering what had become of Lucy.

Lucy had not been home to dinner—

the Coulchers dined in the middle of the day—she had gone out after breakfast to do some shopping, and she had not returned. Mrs. Coulcher was not anxious about Lucy; she was only wondering what had become of her. If it had been Nancy, it would have been different. Her eyes kept straying over to Nancy standing at the window, while she tried to listen to the latest scandal.

The girl at the window was not taking any notice of the people in the room; she did not pretend to take any notice; she stood drumming on the window pane and looking down the street.

She was a tall girl, tall and shapely, her back was to the people in the room, so that only a view of her shoulders could be obtained, and the back of her head. They were strong, shapely young shoulders, and her head was well thrown back, and she had rich brown hair, rich and abundant, with red lights in it, and she wore it in the latest fashion. A little bit of her profile was visible, a dainty profile with a well-marked outline, and thin scarlet lips, thinner lips than most women, and a wider mouth. A mere button hole of a mouth couldn't have shown such a liberal display of lovely little, white, sharp teeth. She was showing her white sharp teeth now, as she stood smiling at the window and looking down the street.

Augusta, who was pouring out the tea at a small table at the other end of the room, saw her smiling, and a cloud came over her plain face, and her hand shook. She very nearly let the cup she was filling brim over.

Augusta was not the least like her sister; she was short and dowdy, and had blunt features, and a great deal of dull, drab, tow-coloured hair, and a wide forehead. Her face was pale and freckled, not nice little freckles, but large patches that gave a decided tone to her complexion. And she had pale blue eyes that very often had red rims round them with reading late.

Augusta was the blue stocking of the family, and she was credited with consuming a great amount of midnight oil.

Augusta was like her mother, whose hair had once been drab, but was now grey, and she was endowed by nature with a blunt profile and mild blue eyes.

One almost wondered, looking at the commonplace mother and daughters, how such a variety as Nancy had crept in.

While Augusta was engaged pouring out that cup of tea, Nancy escaped from the room. She had gone out so quietly, that when Augusta looked up again, she was surprised to see her no longer standing there drumming on the window pane.

She had not time to be surprised for long; there was a ring at the bell, a quiet, assured ring, without the least eagerness or trepidation in it, and a moment or two after, the drawing-room door was thrown open, and some one was announced:

"Mr. Montagu Asquith."

Mrs. Coulcher came forward and greeted her guest; she greeted him with quite tremulous eagerness, and Augusta gave him her hand across the tea table.

There was a vacant chair near the table, and he dropped down into it, and then he looked round the room. He was near sighted, and he had to put up a glass that hung by a thin gold chain, to see clearly to the further end of the room.

Augusta saw the movement and blushed. He was evidently looking round for some one—and—and, it was not for Augusta.

Mr. Montagu Asquith was a brother of the rector of St. Radegund's. He was a great scholar, had taken a Double First at Cambridge, and was a Fellow of his college. He had only quite recently resigned his fellowship and come to Stoke Edith; he had come to settle there, and had bought a house in the neighbourhood in order to be near his brother. He would be a distinct addition to Stoke Edith Society; a man of wealth, and learning, and leisure—and a bachelor.

Perhaps it was this last distinction that made him so interesting to the widows of Stoke Edith—the widows with marriageable daughters—this in connection with his other recommendations.

He was a man of forty, perhaps forty-five; he looked old for his years; and his hair, which was light brown and scanty, was already a little worn on the top. Perhaps this was the result of his immense learning. He had a high, narrow forehead and mild eyes, set rather far back in his head—the eyes of a scholar! His cheeks were hollow like his eyes, with a pink flush on them, and a small, scanty whisker at the side; his mouth, which was large and thin-lipped, was clean-shaven, but he wore a small tuft of hair on his chin.

He was carefully dressed, and had a thick scarf round his neck on this warm April day, and carried a pair of knitted gloves. He looked like a man who had got in the way of taking care of himself.

Augusta enquired after his cough; she had found out that he liked to have his ailments petted and made much of.

The cough had been trying lately, she learnt; the east wind that had prevailed until now hadn't been at all good for it.

"No," he wouldn't take any tea, "thank you;" he had been forbidden by his medical adviser to take tea. His nerves had been a little out of order lately, and tea had been strictly prohibited.

When Augusta had exhausted his cough and his nerves, she asked him how his house was getting on. He was furnishing the house he had lately purchased, and was living at the Rectory until it was ready for occupation.

At the mention of the house, his face lighted up and a warmer colour came into his cheeks.

"That reminds me," he said with some animation, "that I wanted to consult your sister. I wanted to ask her about the kitchen dresser."

"I don't think Nancy knows much about kitchen dressers," Augusta said, rather tartly; she couldn't keep a little sharpness out of her voice, she had no patience with the man. "What did you want to ask her about it?"

"I was in doubt whether it ought to be painted—or—or varnished, or left in its natural state, and—and I thought she would help me to decide. It—it wouldn't do to make a mistake; I — I want everything to be as nearly perfect as possible."

Mr. Montagu Asquith had a slight infirmity in his speech; it was nothing very much, it hardly amounted to a stammer, unless he was unusually excited; it only took the less noticeable form of a slight repetition of a word now and then in a sentence, accompanied by a slight in-drawing of the breath.

It was the penalty he paid for his Double First. A man cannot go into the fray and carry off the laurels of the University unscathed. He had not suffered much, only a scratch; a slight touch of paralysis. Nothing compared to other men, who, as a penalty for their success, sometimes drag a useless leg after them for the remainder of their lives. They may be seen—dozens of them—in every University town, bearing about with them the trophies of their splendid achievements.

"I think Lucy would be the best to ask," Augusta said, referring to the dresser. "Domestic economy is one of her subjects. I believe she is going to lecture on it at Miss Mallet's. We are all going to do something, you know, to help mother. I am going to teach some little boys Latin and Euclid, to prepare them for the grammar school; I have got six pupils already. Nancy is going to give lessons on the violin."

Mr. Asquith's fine countenance paled.

"Give lessons—on—on the vi-o-o-lin!" he repeated, deeply moved.

When he was excited the stammer came in.

"Yes; it is what she can do best," Augusta said with some spirit.

"I hope the occasion will not arrive for —for—for your sister—for Miss Nan—Nan

—Nancy to go out as a teacher!" the scholar said in quite a shocked voice.

Nancy might have been going out as a housemaid for the fuss he made about it. Nancy had slipped out of the room unnoticed when she saw Mr. Asquith coming up the street—she knew exactly what he was coming for.

He was coming to propose.

She read it in his step, in the unwonted flush on his hollow cheeks, in the set of his woollen scarf—he wore it buttoned inside his coat to-day, not outside as he was accustomed to wear it—and in his horrible knitted gloves.

He was wearing a new pair to-day—at least Nancy had not seen him wearing them before—and as he came up the street, with a flush on his thin cheeks and his confident step, she found herself wondering how long they would last, and if she would have to knit the next pair. With this absurd idea in her mind, she turned away with a laugh, and saw the curate of St. Radegund's approaching from an opposite direction. They would hardly meet at the door, she calculated, rapidly measuring the distances with an experienced eye; they would just miss each other, and then with a smile she slipped quietly out of the room.

She need not have been afraid. Mr. Asquith could not have proposed to her before a roomful of people. Besides she could not be *quite* sure that he had worked himself up to the point.

He had been working himself up for some time past. He had been getting nearer and nearer to the point every time he saw her, but the crisis had not yet arrived. He did everything deliberately. He did not approach the subject with unscholarly haste. He felt the ground quite sure under his feet at every step.

He was nearer to-day than he was yesterday, Nancy was quite sure when she saw those new worsted gloves, and then, in a fit of perverseness, she laughed and stole away.

"Show Mr. Craik into the dining-room, Russell," she said to the maid as she crossed the passage, just as her elderly suitor came up the steps.

She laughed and waited while the drawing-room door was opened and shut behind him, and then she went over to the mantel-piece and looked in the glass. Her hair was quite in order, and there was nothing in her dress awry, and the face in the glass smiled brightly back at her. It was not a strictly beautiful face; the features were not regular, and the mouth was much too wide, and the lips too thin and receding. Some day, when she had grown old, and the softness of youth had departed, the piquant nose and chin might become nutcrackers. There was a charm somewhere in the face that was smiling bewitchingly in the glass, although there was no one to smile back, only the portrait of an old man, a commonplace-looking old man, over the sideboard opposite, and the two faces were reflected side by side.

The two faces in the glass were strangely alike—ridiculously alike—though one was old and grey, and red and bloated. A good-tempered, florid old face, with immense bushy eyebrows, and a curious way of screwing up the eyes that stout people sometimes have, and a trick of drawing down the corners of the mouth.

As the faces smiled at each other in the glass the resemblance grew more marked. There was the same damask colour in the cheeks, the same thickly-defined eyebrows and long eyelashes, and the way of drawing the eyelids together, only in Nancy's case the eyelids drooped—there will be time enough for them to screw up by-and-bye—and the same trick of drawing down the corners of the mouth. It was the same face in miniature with the coarseness smoothed out of it, and the defects, which were defects no longer, lending it its peculiar and irresistible charm.

The florid old man over the sideboard was the Reverend Augustus Coulcher, late rector of St. Ninians in Cornwall, and if Mr. Darwin had had the privilege of his acquaintance, and the acquaintance of his beautiful young daughter, he would have built up a lovely theory of evolution—evolution and variation. Distinct variation.

While the faces were still smiling at each other in the glass, the dining-room door was thrown open and the curate of St. Radegund's was announced.

Nancy left off smiling at no one in particular in the glass, and came forward smiling to meet the curate. She had a ready way of blushing, and a delightful smile, and she drew her eyelids together in a bewitching way that made poor Douglas Craik's heart—his much too susceptible heart—go pit-a-pat. It hadn't gone pit-a-pat while he was talking to Lucy, who was worth a dozen of her sister, although she had not inherited the paternal knack of bringing her eyelids together, and the corners of her mouth had not that pathetic droop about them.

It was an absurd thing for a man to be moved by such details, a man who ought to have known better.

Douglas Craik with his heart thumping in that ridiculous manner thought Nancy had put on all those beautiful smiles and blushes for him; he had seen so little of women, he knew so little about them. He was quite ready to be taken in by any syren with long-lashed grey eyes, and a pretty drooping mouth.

"I hear you are going to give lessons on the violin at Miss Mallet's," he said awkwardly. "I met your sister this morning, and she told me all about it. I am so sorry that the necessity should have arisen. It is very brave of you."

Nancy laughed. She had a dear little laugh.

"Oh, I shan't mind giving lessons on the violin," she said gaily, "I love the violin. I never get tired of playing it, and I am only to teach two hours a day, ten till twelve. Lucy will have the whole morning engaged, and Augusta, I'm afraid Augusta will have to give up both mornings and afternoons. She is going to teach a class of little boys, to prepare them for the school."

She spoke so gaily of the programme she and her sisters had undertaken, that the explanation of that pathetic droop of the corners of the mouth that he had remarked the night before, when he thought every minute Nancy was going to cry, was clearly not to be found here.

He had called to-day expressly to offer his sympathy. It was the only thing he was good at; offering sympathy and counsel and spiritual comfort to any one who happened to be in need of them.

Nancy Coulcher did not look the least like needing anything in that way, as she stood smiling down upon him.

He was such a little fellow, and he looked shorter by comparison as he stood on the hearthrug beside her; she had not asked him to sit down. Her lusty health and strength seemed to make his weakness more apparent, to dwarf him, and make him look smaller and slighter. He had looked ever so much more dignified in the pulpit, she remarked as she looked down upon him standing there. He was seen at his best, his very best, in the chancel of St. Radegund's, with the high light from the east window streaming down on his pale, clear-cut face. It was no wonder that all the girls in Stoke Edith were raving about him.

He ought to have gone about all day in his cassock and surplice, not in that ridiculous short jacket and limp felt hat.

"I'm afraid Mrs. Coulcher is in trouble about your brother at Cambridge," he said, blushing at his own temerity. "I hope it is not true that he is going to be 'sent down'?"

"I hope not. His tutor is very angry with him; he has threatened to send him down. It will be a great expense to mother if he does, and he will lose the term. He has been idle and extravagant; he is always getting into trouble. It is a great pity mother ever let him go up to Cambridge."

"It will be a great thing for him to take

a degree. It means so much in life; it is worth making a sacrifice for. Your mother was quite right to let him go; we must all pray for him that he may be kept," he said earnestly. He was sorry for the mother and the girls, and the anxiety this good-for-nothing brother was giving them, but he knew no other remedy for their trouble than prayer. It was his sole prescription.

"Oh, mother is always praying for him," Nancy said with a gay little laugh, "and it doesn't seem to do any good."

While they were talking there had been another ring at the front door bell, and someone came hurriedly into the room. It was Lucy, who had just got away from Sarah Strong, and had come in here thinking the room was empty. She was white and tired, and there was a strained look about her eyes, and her lips were trembling.

"Wherever have you been, Lucy?"

Nancy was standing between the door and the fireplace, and the girl did not see the curate standing there. Lucy was tired and overdone, and she threw herself on a couch that stood near the door and began to cry hysterically.

She did not attempt to answer her sister's question, she only sat there crying and making a spectacle of herself, while Nancy stood looking at her with an air of mild surprise and wonder. She did not fly over to Lucy's side and take off her hat and smooth back her hair and strive to comfort her in sweet, sisterly fashion; she stood smiling down at the curate, and wondering why Lucy was making herself so foolish.

"I'm afraid you've been doing too much, Miss Lucy," he said; he knew exactly how she felt, he often wanted, after a long morning's visiting, to throw himself down somewhere and have a good cry. He was a poor weak fellow, he hadn't the backbone for a curate.

Lucy looked up when she heard his voice, and hurriedly dried her eyes.

"I have been sitting with Sarah Strong," she said, " and the room was so close."

"You have not been sitting with her since—since I saw you this morning?"

"Ye—es, I have been sitting with her ever since."

"So long?" he said, and his face flushed, and he forgot all about Nancy, and came over to the couch where Lucy was sitting.

"You have been with her all these hours—you have been able to do something with her? You have succeeded where I have failed. Oh, I am so thankful you have succeeded at last!"

"I have not been able to do anything with her," Lucy said, hanging her head.

"Not anything?—and you have been with her so long! You have been able to read to her?"

"She would not let me read a single word."

"Then you have prayed with her; she can sometimes bear a prayer when she cannot listen to a text."

"She would not let me pray with her."

"And she kept you there so long? It was a great opportunity."

There was a note of disappointment, almost reproof in his voice, that stung Lucy like a blow, and she kept her tears back with an effort.

"She is an old woman," she said quickly, with her lips trembling, "and she has had a great many troubles; she has not been free from pain for years. She is weary of groaning and praying, she has been praying for years and years, and she is none the better. Oh! you must not judge her by the same standard as other people."

"I should be very sorry to judge her," the Curate said meekly. "I should be glad to do her good if I could; I have been visiting her for months, and it is always the same tale; she is too ill to bear any reading, and she can't listen to any prayers. Poor old woman! Perhaps the fault is in me. I have not been praying for her as I ought."

He went away humbled and saddened: he was sure he had failed in his duty; he would not go into the other room and have a cup of tea. He promised to come and see Mrs. Coulcher another day, and he went away to pray for Nancy's good-for-nothing brother, and old bed-ridden Sarah Strong.

He was always praying for somebody or other: worldly people used to say jocosely that it was his meat and drink:

perhaps it was: he was such a puny little fellow to do so much work, to be consumed with such untiring energies, he must have had some secret source of supply.

Lucy Coulcher was dreadfully ashamed of herself for breaking down, for that ridiculous exhibition, as Nancy feelingly termed it; she had no idea that Mr. Craik was there, or she wouldn't have given free course to those foolish tears for the world.

That visit to Sarah Strong had upset her more than she cared to acknowledge. She had been brooding over all sorts of dreadful things while she had been sitting in that darkened room. She had been questioning the ways of Providence: she had been driven face to face with solemn, aching, anxious problems, and she had not been able to solve them.

Her faith, her calm, assured faith, had never been disturbed until to-day, and now all sorts of dreadful unspoken doubts kept surging up in her mind. Was there any use in praying after all? Oh! it was a dreadful question. Was it Providence or chance that ruled in the world?—and why were the burdens that were laid on mankind, so unequal—so terribly unequal?

What had that poor old soul groaning from morning till night on her bed of pain done that she should suffer so horribly?—and what had she herself done, that all that women most prize in the world, beauty, and admiration, and love, should be denied her, and that Nancy should have all—everything—full measure of this world's good, pressed down, running over? Oh, what had she done that there should be this disparity in their lot?

Lucy could not find an answer to any of these foolish questions that had arisen in her mind, as she sat with the old woman's hand in hers in that darkened room.

Perhaps she will find an answer to them by-and-bye. There are some questions that can never be answered, some perplexing doubts that can never be solved—else, where were faith?

CHAPTER III.

NEARER AND NEARER.

"Men's love, and birds' love,
And women's love and men's!"

WHEN the people had gone away, Mr. Montagu Asquith among them, Augusta told Nancy about the kitchen dresser.

"He must be in earnest, or he wouldn't want you to decide about the dresser," Augusta said with a sigh.

"Of course he's in earnest," Lucy said quickly, with the colour coming into her pale face as she spoke; "he wouldn't come here day after day, as he does, and pay Nan such marked attention, if he were not in earnest. I think it's coming nearer and nearer."

"It's a long time coming," Nancy said with a laugh, "the longer the better.

What a Molly he must be to trouble himself about the kitchen dresser! I suppose he will ask me to choose the saucepans next!"

Nancy tossed her head and went out of the room singing, and presently they heard her thrumming gaily on the fiddle in the adjoining room.

She had everything to sing for. The cloud that hung over the house didn't overshadow her, didn't darken her bright horizon. She had youth, health, abundant health, immense vitality and capacity for enjoyment, and lovers by the score.

The last thing in the world she wanted was a husband. Of course she would have one by-and-bye, when the game was played out, but now, in the midst of life, when the world was at her feet, the little, tiny world of Stoke Edith, marriage was the very, very last thing to be thought of.

"Stupid old frump!" Nancy Coulcher

said to herself as she crossed the hall, "what can he expect me to care about kitchen dressers?" and then she took up her fiddle and began to play a dance tune.

"I wish Mr. Asquith would come to the point," Lucy said crossly, when she had left the room. "If Nancy were once engaged—openly engaged, there would be an end of all this nonsense. I should make it a point to tell everybody directly. I don't think it fair of her to encourage half-a-dozen men that she doesn't care a straw for, when she is already as good as engaged to another man. It's mean, and cruel, and heartless."

Lucy spoke with some heat, and there was an unwonted colour in her cheeks, and her lips were trembling.

Augusta raised her eyes from the book she was reading, and looked at Lucy keenly. Her eyes were very mild blue eyes, but they saw a long way; the boys used to say they could see through a stone wall.

"Who is it now?" she asked.

"Oh, you needn't ask! I should have thought you could have seen it last night. He never took his eyes off our pew all through the sermon, and this morning, when I met him in Silver Street, the first question he asked was after Nancy; and when I came in this afternoon they were alone together in the dining-room."

"You — don't — mean Mr. Craik?" Augusta gasped; she did not often gasp, she was not an emotional young woman, but she gasped now.

"Who else should I mean?" Lucy said tartly.

"I—I thought it was you!" Augusta answered meekly.

"Me!" Lucy exclaimed, flushing up scarlet like a poppy.

She was a poor-spirited little thing, and she was overdone. Sitting in that cramped position by the bedside of a dreadful old woman all those hours had been too much for her nerves, and she broke down all at once and began to cry.

"Oh, no, he never thought of me!" poor Lucy sobbed. She was very angry with herself for crying, but the tears would not be kept back. Her little castle had just crumbled away and vanished, and she could not help weeping over it.

"I am sure Mr. Craik admired you very much when he first came here. He told mother that he didn't know how he should get on without you in the parish," Augusta said by way of comfort; she couldn't think of anything else to say.

"Oh, that's quite another thing," Lucy interrupted impatiently. "He doesn't admire Nancy in that way. He—*he loves Nancy.*"

"Then I'm very sorry for him!" Augusta said, closing her book with a bang, "he ought to know better. I've no patience with men, sensible men like Mr. Craik, who know, or who profess to know so much about human nature and the higher life, and all that sort of thing, being caught by such shallow tricks as Nancy's!"

"He is only like the rest," Lucy sobbed.

Augusta was very angry. She thought so much of the Curate of St. Radegund's.

"He ought not to be like the rest!" she said, puckering her forehead, and drawing her thick drab eyebrows together—they were bushy eyebrows like her father's, only they were drab. "I'm dreadfully disappointed in him! I expected so much better things of him! I thought, with all he has gone through in that dreadful London slum—after all the work he has done, the beautiful real work, and all the lessons he has learnt there, after having been brought face to face with the realities of life; having gone through so much and found out for himself what is real and abiding, and what is false and hollow, having found out all this, and realised it, to fall *so* low. Oh! I have no patience with him!"

Augusta was very angry.

Perhaps she was right; the Curate of St. Radegund's ought to have known better. What is the use of preaching to other people about self-discipline and self-restraint, and all that sort of thing if a man is not master of himself?

Nancy Coulcher began her violin lessons at Miss Mallet's school the next day. "St. John's in the Wilderness," as Miss Mallet's establishment was called, was situated at the other end of Stoke Edith. The grammar school, which had recently been rebuilt, and removed a mile out of the town, lay beyond it. It was not Miss

Mallet's fault that the grammar school was in her immediate neighbourhood. The undesirable propinquity was none of her seeking.

If the trustees of the old foundation chose to carry the school out of the town, where it had flourished for over two centuries, and set it down at her back door, they must take the consequences.

St. John's in the Wilderness had enjoyed a high repute in the county as a first-class boarding school for girls fifty years before there was any talk of removing the grammar school. It would not enjoy it much longer, parents had already begun to talk of taking away their girls. They could not go outside the gates of the Wilderness now for their long country walks without encountering the boarders; and they could not walk in an opposite direction without meeting the day boys, coming or going to and from the school, and the junior masters trooping up from their lodgings in the town.

Lucy, who went to the Wilderness early, and came back late, missed the troop of boys going up from the town; it was generally a noisy party, and she was glad to miss them. She had her lesson to think about on the way, and she could not think with a lot of boys shouting, and racing up the hill like a lot of mad things all round her.

It was unfortunate that Nancy should have to go alone; but Mrs. Coulcher comforted herself with the thought that she could go with the boys, and come back with the boys. It would really be company for her.

Nancy didn't go with the boys after that first morning. They were in such a desperate hurry to reach the school, though the bell had not begun to ring, when they reached the foot of the hill, that they started off at a run, and left her to walk the rest of the way alone. That is, not quite alone: one of the masters walked up the hill beside her to the gate of the Wilderness, and by a strange chance, he joined her at the same spot, when she was coming back after the lesson.

The Curate met them coming back; he had remembered suddenly, just before twelve o'clock, that he had a visit to make in the neighbourhood of the Wilderness, and he had started off up the hill with his heart beating pit-a-pat and a ridiculous pink colour in his face. He saw Nancy and the schoolmaster coming gaily down the hill when he was half-way up, and he could do nothing less than go on his way, as if the meeting were purely accidental.

It was Gilbert Earle, the mathematical master, he remarked, who was coming down the hill with Nancy, and he was carrying her fiddle. Of course if he had happened to have been in time to walk back with her, he would have been expected to carry the fiddle. The mathematical tutor was not the least like the little slender curate; he was a head and shoulders above him; tall and handsome and black-bearded; no girl in her senses would have hesitated between them.

Nancy's face was flushed and smiling, she was blushing divinely he saw as he passed her, and went on his solitary way. The cloud he had seen on her face in church on Sunday, had quite passed away; it had nothing at any rate to do with the teaching at the Wilderness, or with Geoffrey's trouble.

It was nothing unusual to see Gilbert Earle talking to Nancy Coulcher. All the masters at the grammar school, that is, all the unmarried masters, were in love with her, and she encouraged them all alike; she made no difference. It did not very much matter to Nancy which it was; the tall wrangler, or the short classic; the fierce-looking German, who was the professor of modern languages, or the mild-eyed botanist who taught Natural Science. She bewitched them all with the same looks and the same tones, and misled them with the same misleading smiles. She took them all in. She liked above all things to be admired, and she unconsciously, with a quite artless art, sought to win and charm every foolish young man that she met. She was not handicapped by any ridiculous delicacy of feeling.

She began by liking all her admirers universally, and, by-and-bye, when the novelty wore off, and she got a little tired of so much admiration, she began to pick and choose. She had weeded out a good many; she had begun to pick and choose.

She had picked out Gilbert Earle from the number, and a classical master, who had sailed for India a month ago—she had a letter from him in her pocket at that moment—and Mr. Asquith.

She had picked out these three; she had not included the curate in this inner circle of first favourites, and she had to choose between them.

The choice could not be far off; not so far off as she desired, at least so it seemed when she got back after that first morning's teaching.

Augusta met her in the hall when she came in flushed and smiling.

"Mamma wants you in the drawing-room, Nan," she said in a mysterious voice. "You are to go to her before you take off your things."

Nancy went in gaily—to be more correct she bounced into the room, but her face fell when she saw a letter on the table before her mother, a letter in a handwriting she knew well.

Mrs. Coulcher took up the letter nervously, and gave it to Nancy. Her fingers were trembling the girl noticed when she gave it to her.

"It is from Mr. Asquith, Nancy; he left it himself. He called soon after you had gone, and—and asked for you, and when he found you were not at home, he left the letter."

"Whatever can he want to write to me about?" Nan said flippantly, and she began to tear open the letter.

"I think you had better read it in—in your own room, my dear. Take it upstairs, and read it by yourself. Remember it is only written for your eyes."

Nancy took the letter upstairs with her.

"I expect it is only about the kitchen dresser," she said, in a most unfeeling way.

She did not come down stairs for a long time; not until after Lucy had come back, and the dinner gong had sounded. She came down stairs whistling—she was a wonderful whistler—and she took her seat at the dinner table. She did not notice that they were all looking at her, and that her mother was so nervous that she could hardly carve the leg of mutton.

"Well?" Lucy said in a whisper when the servant had left the room.

"Well?" Augusta repeated breathlessly.

Mrs. Coulcher did not say "Well?"— not audibly, but she paused with her knife in the joint, and the gravy running out, while the three red-headed boys round the table—they had all red hair, like their father, stopped talking and wondered when their dinner was coming.

Mrs. Coulcher lifted up her eyes to the portrait of her deceased husband over the sideboard. It was a supreme moment.

The Rev. Augustus keeping guard over the pickles and the jam, seemed to be screwing his eyelids together and whispering a ghostly "Well?"

Nancy laughed.

"What do you mean?" she said, "why are you all looking at me?"

"Is—is it all settled?" Lucy said eagerly, with a little break in her voice.

"Settled?—what settled?"

"Mr. Asquith's letter," Augusta said solemnly, "it has taken you a long time to read it."

"Oh, I had forgotten all about it," Nancy said laughing, and she took the crumpled letter out of her pocket and tossed it across the table to Augusta; "you can read it if you like; there's a message for you in it."

Augusta read it with her tell-tale face growing white and red by turns, and when she had finished she put it back in the envelope.

"Mr. Asquith has asked Nancy and me to go up and look at his new house this afternoon, mother," she said meekly. "His sister is going up with him at three o'clock, and he has asked us to join them there, and walk back to the rectory to tea."

"I said it was getting nearer and nearer," Lucy said solemnly.

Mrs. Coulcher's face fell, and she went on carving the leg of mutton.

"If—if Mr. Asquith's sister is there I suppose you can go," she said stiffly, "but I think he ought to have asked me."

She was just a little disappointed. She had made up her mind it was an offer.

CHAPTER IV.

LADYLIFT.

"Go not, happy day,
 Till the maiden yields."

THE inspection of Ladylift, Mr. Asquith's new house, was quite satisfactory. Nancy went over it that afternoon from garret to basement. She didn't tear through it, as she generally tore through things she didn't care much about. She went through it conscientiously, opening the doors of all the cupboards, examining the kitchen range, peering into the pantries and cellars and deciding the vexed question of the kitchen dresser.

Mr. Asquith went through it with her, explaining everything to her, and consulting her about the furniture. It might have been a settled thing. They might have been engaged for months, and were on the eve of setting up housekeeping.

It really was, as Lucy said, "getting nearer and nearer."

He might have proposed to her then, in one of those empty rooms; he had plenty of opportunities; in the attics with the sloping roofs, where in one corner Nancy could scarcely stand upright—they had gone up alone to the attics. Miss Asquith was a stout lady, rather short in the breath, and she declined to go a step farther than the second floor, and Augusta stayed behind to keep her company.

Nancy and her lover were so long upstairs in that empty attic, they had quite time enough to settle the matter—time and opportunity. Augusta thought it was all over when she saw them coming down the narrow staircase. Nancy in her best frock, with her brown hair with the red tints in it, all ablaze with the sunlight that poured down upon it from the skylight in the roof, and her bright face all aglow. She looked so happy and radiant, she might have been descending from the clouds.

"Am I to congratulate you?" Augusta asked her when they had got a moment together. She could not ask the question quite steadily, she could not keep a quiver out of her voice.

"Congratulate me! What for?"

"Oh, I thought it was settled! you were so long up there."

"We were looking out of the window; there is a lovely view from that attic window."

Nancy saw everything; the beautiful great house, the stables and coach-house —there was room enough for two carriages, she remarked in the coach-house, a brougham and a pony carriage, and stabling for half-a-dozen horses, and a harness room. The accommodation was excellent. Augusta hadn't much interest in the stables, and Miss Asquith preferred the greenhouses, and Nancy and her lover went through them alone.

There was ample opportunity for Mr. Asquith to propose; he could have proposed in the loose box, which Nancy would insist on going in. He would never find a better chance.

He let the opportunity slip, as he had let the chance in the attics slip; perhaps he thought the surroundings were unworthy. Nancy was smiling upon him, and the hour was propitious, but he let it slip.

They went through the gardens together in the sweet Spring sunshine. Everything was breaking into bud and blossom. The chestnuts overhead had already burst through their pale pink sheaths, they would be blossoming presently, and the lilac was already purple overhead, and the pear trees were in their white. There was a fragrance of violets and hyacinths and sweet-smelling Spring flowers in the borders, and the meadows beyond were green with the new green of the year, and the sky was blue overhead.

Nancy and her lover walked together through the green alleys, between the fragrant borders, with the branches meeting above and the sunlight dropping down on their path. It was a lovely opportunity; he would never have such another.

Nancy thought he was her Fate, and she was ready—quite ready—to accept him. How could she do otherwise, after going through the house and the stables, the sight of that loose box had moved her deeply. She was fond of riding, she loved it above everything. When she had a horse of her own, she had always told herself it should have a loose box. She was like the Queen of Sheba, she had seen so much, she had no spirit left in her to say " No."

If Mr. Asquith had asked her to-day, he would have had a favourable answer.

The afternoon went on, and the golden atmosphere of enchantment faded, and the mists from the valley—Stoke Edith lay in a valley—rose up to meet them as they walked back to the rectory to tea. Nancy's smiles were gone; her low replies were silenced: the opportunity was lost; the happy, happy moment was gone for ever.

" What is in those big cases ? " she asked him as they passed through the hall when they were going away.

" They are the cases containing my specimens," he said. " They are not unpacked yet ; when they are unpacked I am promising myself great pleasure in going through them with you. I have some specimens of coleoptera that are rare in private collections, that are almost unique. You are fond of entomology, I think?"

"I love it!" Nancy said with rapture. She wasn't thinking very much of what she was saying. She was wondering why Augusta and Miss Asquith were lagging behind.

"I'm very glad; I was not sure whether it was botany or entomology you were fond of. I knew it was one of the two; your mother was telling me you had taken it up as a pet study."

"Oh, that was botany, but I like both. I pressed a lot of flowers last year, and I helped the boys arrange their butterflies. I love butterflies."

Mr. Asquith smiled, a gentle, superior, patronising smile, and looked at the bright face of the girl by his side. It was really worth looking at. Nancy had always a delightful colour, and her profile was charming; he had never remarked until to-day how blue her eyes were, blue as the

April skies above. He was smiling at her ignorance—her ignorance and innocence; he would not have had her a bit wiser for the world! He was picturing to himself all through that walk back to the rectory, when he ought to have been making love, how delightful it would be to instruct her in the mysteries of *Lepidoptera*, and *Neuroptera*, and *Coleoptera*, in the future. What a happy, happy time lay before him! He was glad that Nancy was an enthusiast; it would make the task so much easier; she had so much to learn; it would take him a life-time to teach her that botany did not wholly consist in pressing flowers, or entomology in setting butterflies.

When Nancy got back to Cherry Garden she was not in the best of tempers. She was angry, and disappointed, and bored to death with *Coleoptera*. There was a case of beetles at the rectory, and her lover had insisted on going through them, teaching her their long, dreadful Latin names.

"Oh, dear no, he hasn't proposed, and he isn't going to!" she said in answer to Lucy's tender inquiry, as she was taking off her things. Lucy was very anxious that Mr. Asquith should propose; she couldn't understand what he was waiting for.

"I made sure that he would propose to-day," she said, blushing guiltily as she spoke. "I was so sure—that—that I told Mr. Craik you were engaged."

"You told Mr. Craik I was engaged!" Nancy said in an awful voice, and she took little Lucy by the shoulder and turned her face round to the light.

"Why did you tell him that lie?" she demanded fiercely.

Her blue eyes were blazing with passion, and her cheeks were crimson, and her lips were quivering.

Lucy cowered before her; she never remembered having been afraid of Nancy before.

"I did not think there was any harm," she said meekly. "I thought, I made sure he was going to ask you to-day. Why should he ask you to look at his house, and consult you about the furniture, if—if he didn't intend to ask you to marry him?"

"You had no right to say I was engaged if he had asked me," Nancy said, not a bit mollified by Lucy's miserable explanation. "I don't know that I shall accept him if he does. I don't know why you are all in such a hurry to get rid of me. I shall take my time. I am not going to be forced into marrying anybody. There are a dozen men in Stoke Edith ready— dying to marry me, and—and I am going to take my choice."

Nancy was as good as her word. She refused to see Mr. Asquith when he called the next day. He had brought a book on beetles for her to read, and he left it with a message—a message and a note. The message was to the effect that he would call at the same hour on the following day, and that he hoped he would find her at home; and the letter—well, it was a ridiculous letter for a lover to write; it was all about beetles, and the pleasure with which he was looking forward to devote the remainder of his life to instructing Nancy in their ways and habits. He proposed to himself the agreeable task of forming her mind, and he was going to begin with beetles. He couldn't begin much lower.

That letter settled his fate.

Nancy met the Curate of St. Radegund's as she came back from Miss Mallet's that morning. She did not go to the Wilderness through the town to-day, with all the grammar school boys at her heels. She went by way of the meadows, which was a quieter way, but at least half a mile farther. She had to start earlier in the morning, and she came back later at noon, and she very seldom came back alone. It was on her way back that she met the Curate. She had not seen him, except in church, since the day she met him coming down the hill with one of the masters. She had given the masters the slip, or she would have had one of them with her now; they were always making little schemes to walk back with her.

She had given them the slip to-day, and she had left her fiddle behind; she was sauntering across the meadow alone when the Curate met her. He saw her quite a long way off in her pretty Spring frock, with the round sailor hat showing off the lovely oval of her face, and the warm tints in her brown hair, gleaming like burnished gold in the sun. He had never seen her look so sweet before, so sweet and simple, and womanly. He clasped his hands, as he had a habit of doing, as he saw her coming towards him, and waited for her at the stile. He could do nothing less; he could not go on, and let her get over the stile by herself.

A few days ago he would have fancied as he waited there, that it was his Fate coming towards him, but Lucy's words were still ringing in his ears. They had not been out of them, indeed, since that unlucky afternoon. He could hear them quite plainly as Nancy came smiling across the grass.

"My sister is engaged; she is going to marry Mr. Asquith."

He was repeating them drearily to himself as Nancy came up to the stile.

"Oh, I am so glad to see you, Mr. Craik," she began, and then she stopped and blushed.

"I wanted to see you so much—I—I wanted to tell you——"

There was a delicious little tremor in her voice that he had never remarked in it before.

It was rather difficult to go on; she didn't know how hard it was, until she stood there beside the stile, with Douglas Craik looking at her with his earnest eyes that seemed to pierce her little shallow soul. She was very glad the stile was between them.

"What did you want to tell me?" he said, when he found she did not go on. He thought it was something about the parish, about Lucy, about that tiresome old Sarah Strong, who was always sending for him, and wouldn't hear a word he said when he came to her. There was no eagerness in his voice, no expectation in his eyes; he was watching her, as he had a habit of watching everybody, as she spoke to him, and he was wondering what a girl like this could find in Montagu Asquith.

"Oh!" she said drooping her head rosily, and crushing with her heel the flowers that were crowding up round the stile, "it is about Mr. Asquith; Lucy told you something—yesterday—there is no truth in it—it is a mistake."

It was very prettily done. She was so confused, and her lips were trembling, and there was a little throaty quaver in her voice that touched him, that moved him out of himself. It was quite as well that Nancy did not look up, that she was engaged in crushing those wretched daisy buds that came in her way into the earth; she would have seen, if she had looked up at that moment, that a flame had leaped into Douglas Craik's eyes, and that they were blazing upon her with—well, with a look that she would not have mistaken.

"It was a mistake then?" he said in a voice he could scarcely keep steady.

"It was quite a mistake. I—I have no intention of marrying Mr. Asquith."

His face flushed and faded; his eyes brightened and darkened.

"Your sister told me it was settled; that you had gone to look over his house——" he faltered; he could not keep his voice steady.

"I went with his sister to see the gardens, and we came back to the rectory to tea, and he showed me his beetles—you know his beetles, Mr. Craik. Oh, how I hate those beetles!"

She ground her heel into the unoffending daisies in the grass as if they were the beetles, and she looked up into his face, with the corners of her mouth drawn down in that pretty pathetic way she had, looking childish, and troubled, and about to cry.

He would have given the world to have taken her in his arms and told her that Mr. Asquith and his beetles should never, never trouble her again. Fortunately the stile was between them.

"I am very glad it was a mistake," he said huskily; it was all he could find to say, though his heart was thumping dreadfully, and then he had to help her over the stile and walk back with her. He quite forgot where he was going, and he walked all the way back with Nancy, until he came in sight of Cherry Garden.

Douglas Craik was immensely relieved; he really didn't know whether he was on his head or his heels, as he walked back to his lodgings to dinner. He quite forgot that parochial visit he was going to make when he met her; it slipped quite out of his mind. He could think of nothing but Nancy. He was so full of her sweet confidence, of the words she had dropped in her agitation.

Her shy, sad glances had thrilled him with love, pity, and sympathy. He was quite sure that her family were urging her on to this sacrifice. He had heard of Mrs. Coulcher's losses, and Geoffrey's extravagance, and this angel—he called her an angel—this meek, suffering Saint was to be offered up a patient, uncomplaining sacrifice to Moloch!

Mr. Asquith and his beetles were Moloch.

CHAPTER V.

PARADISE.

> "Be near me when the sensuous frame
> Is rack'd with pangs that conquer trust."

Lucy Coulcher went to see poor old Sarah Strong that afternoon. Her visits to Sarah Strong were undertaken rather in the form of a penance. She particularly disliked sitting by the hour in that dark, stuffy room, listening to the groans and complaints of the cantankerous old woman. She could do her no good, she could only listen to her complaints; it was only as a matter of duty she went to see her at all, of duty and of penance. When she had done anything that she thought deserved a specially severe form of penance, she went to Paradise, and sat an hour or two with Sarah Strong.

She was sitting with her that afternoon when the curate came in, and Sarah was holding her hand, as she had held it on that morning when she had sapped all the energy out of her, and she had gone home and had a fit of hysterics.

Lucy looked up when she heard the curate's step on the stairs outside; the room was so dark or he would have seen the sudden colour leap into her pale cheeks when he entered the room. He did not see her at first in the obscurity of that dim room, and with the poor old figure propped up in the bed between them. Lucy would have taken her hand away, and made room for him at the bedside, but the old woman would not release her.

"No, dearie, you mustn't go yet. I couldn' gi'e you up yet; I was jest beginnin' to feel a little easy. I'm allers easier if I've got a hand to hold to."

There really seemed to be something in

what the old woman said; she was not groaning, the curate remarked, when he came up the stairs!

"You here!" he said, when he saw Lucy Coulcher sitting by the bedside holding the old woman's hand.

There was something in the tone in which he said those two words that Lucy didn't like. There was a note of surprise and distrust in them, that pierced her little tender soul, and she drew back into the shadow, with the old woman's hand still clinging to her. She would not let it go.

Douglas Craik had not come to see Lucy, he had come to see Sarah Strong. He had come to administer comfort and consolation, and to illumine with faith and hope the dark way she would shortly have to tread. She turned a deaf ear to his words of comfort, and she declined to see a ray of light, to see a spark indeed. She did nothing but groan and murmur all the time he was in the room.

"I can't hear a word!" she moaned, when he took out his little pocket Bible and read a few verses to her. "I be worse than ever to-day, an' my hearin's most a-gone!"

Douglas Craik read the portion of Scripture he had selected to read to her, whether she heard him or not; he read it unmoved to the end, while the poor old creature on the bed mumbled and groaned, and vowed she couldn't hear a word. When he had finished the portion, he closed the book and went on his knees beside the bed and prayed aloud, and Lucy knelt down beside him.

"I can't bear no prayin'," the old woman whimpered, "it allus upsets me. I'm past bearin' it. The Lord knows how I've a-prayed for years an' years! He knows I be past it now."

The curate went on praying whether the old lady could bear it or not, and when he had finished he got up from his knees. It did not really seem worth while to take so much trouble with an old woman who refused to listen to a word he said, and who was too obstinate to say " Amen " to his petitions.

" I ought not to have told you what I did about Nancy, Mr. Craik," Lucy said timidly, as he was going away, " it was rather premature. You must defer your congratulations for a day or two."

" I shall certainly defer them until your sister tells me I am at liberty to offer them," he said coldly, and then he bowed and went away.

He didn't offer to shake hands with Lucy, she couldn't have shaken hands with him if he had, seeing that Sarah Strong had possessed herself of her right hand, and didn't mean to give it up for another hour.

The tears sprang to Lucy's eyes; she wasn't used to being scolded and snubbed. Of course she had been in the wrong to tell him that Nancy was engaged, before Mr. Asquith had proposed. She had made sure that he was going to ask her that afternoon; it had been getting nearer and nearer, as she expressed it, every day, and she thought the climax had come at last. It could only be a matter of days, hours. Most likely he was proposing to her now. She had left him at Cherry Garden talking to her mother, and Nancy was smiling upon him. She smiled upon every man, but it was not every man, especially in Stoke Edith, where the masters who were in love with her, were all young and struggling for a place on the ladder—it was not everyone who had a beautiful house, and carriages, and horses, and a handsome income to offer her.

Lucy was vexed and angry with herself,

she felt so small and miserable that she couldn't keep her tears back. There was no one to see them here, and she let them fall silently on the bed, at least, she thought they were falling on the bed, but one or two dropped on the old woman's hand.

"He's bin a-scoldin' you, has he?" Sarah Strong said indignantly. She was not past standing up for her friends. "It's about all they parsons are good for. Ratin' an' scoldin' poor folks for not being better nor angels. I should like to see an angel go through what I've a-gone through! Lie awake night after night, an' never a minit wi'out pain, an' bear it patient! Never you mind, dearie, he'll get his reward!"

When Lucy got back to Cherry Garden Mr. Asquith had gone. He had only just gone. He had spent the afternoon with Mrs. Coulcher and Nancy. He had not come empty-handed; he had brought Nancy another book, a book on botany this time, a delightful book full of long Latin names and coloured plates of flowers. There was not a picture worth looking at in it, Nancy declared, as she turned it over impatiently when he was gone; there were only ridiculous bits of flowers, that were about as interesting as his beetles.

He had spent two hours in Nancy's society to-day, and he had not yet asked her the important question.

He had asked her several questions during those two hours that had a bearing on the point; he had asked her whether she preferred oak to mahogany for the dining-room furniture, and he had consulted her about the prevailing colour of the appointments of the drawing-room. To both these important matters Nancy had given her attention. She had settled that oak was more desirable than mahogany for the dining-room, and that terra cotta, pale—pale terra cotta, with a touch of warmth in it, was the most delightful tone for a drawing-room looking out upon a green garden. She had gone so far as to get out her colour box and decide upon the exact shade—there are so many shades in terra cotta—and Mr. Asquith had folded the paper up and put it in his pocket.

It was certainly getting, as Lucy said, " nearer and nearer."

He had asked Nancy before he went away, if he could see her alone the next day, if she would give him an interview, and he had asked her to name the time. She had not named any time, but she had intimated to him that she would be at home all the afternoon, and then she had gone into raptures with his book.

She had been called away from the room for a few minutes while he was there, at least she had gone down the garden to gather some roses and she hadn't come back, and Mr. Asquith had taken the opportunity to speak to her mother.

It is rather an old-fashioned thing to "ask mamma" now-a-days. Mamma is generally consulted when things are quite settled. Nancy's elderly lover was old-fashioned, and he went about everything in a deliberate and ceremonious way.

"You may have noticed—remarked, Mrs. Coulcher," he began in his dry, wordy, pompous fashion, "that your daughter, your youngest daughter, Miss Nancy, is, or rather, has been an—an object—of—of considerable interest to—to me."

It was very hard to get out, much harder than he had expected.

Mrs. Coulcher inclined her head; she did not help him in the least, and there followed an awkward pause. It would be time enough for her to speak when he came to the point.

His throat seemed to give him a good

deal of trouble, it had been rather relaxed lately; he had left off his woollen comforter too early, and he was conscious that for the last five minutes Nancy had left the door open behind her. He had been sitting in a draught.

"The—the time has come, Mrs. Coulcher," he said, clearing his throat, "when I feel it—it—is my duty to speak to you—to—to explain the state of my feelings, and to—ahem!" his throat was getting worse and worse—"to ask your permission, to get your sanction, to my paying my addresses to—to your daughter."

The murder was out, and Nancy's lover sat—not hot and fainting—shivering in the draught. It was as much as he could do to keep himself from getting up and closing that door. It would have been hardly lover-like to have got up at that critical moment.

Mrs. Coulcher remembered her own

youth. Her thoughts went back to that distant day when the Rev. Augustus had wooed her in a somewhat different fashion. It was all a question of temperament. Augustus, if his portrait over the sideboard in the dining-room did him justice, had been red-headed, and of a more fiery nature than this ceremonious wooer.

"I need not tell you, I'm sure, Mr. Asquith," the widow murmured with a sigh —it is always becoming to sigh at such moments, it expresses a gentle reluctance— "that I can have no personal objection to you as a suitor for my dear child's hand. She is very young and thoughtless, but she has the best heart in the world, and has been carefully trained. She is not so domesticated as Augusta and Lucy, but she will learn as she grows older, and—and I think she has the qualities that would make a home happy——"

What more could a mother say?

"Then—then I have your consent to—to ask your daughter—to ask Miss Nancy to be my wife?" the elderly lover said eagerly. He was in a hurry to get the interview over. He was catching a dreadful cold in that draught.

Mrs. Coulcher murmured a tremulous assent. It would be a great thing for the boys, she told herself; and Nancy could not expect to do better, but she would rather he had chosen Augusta.

When Mr. Asquith came the next day Nancy was not at home to receive him, but she had left a missive with the servant who opened the door to him, explaining that she had forgotten yesterday, when she said she would be at home, she had an engagement—a previous engagement.

He read the dear little scented note on the doorstep, and put it in his pocket over his heart, while the maid waited. He had brought Nancy another book on his favourite subject, which he left with a message that he would call at the same hour the next day.

Nancy made a little *moue* when she opened the book, and put it on the shelf with the others—her own little bookshelf in the drawing-room — with her school prizes, and quite a collection of volumes of poetry her lovers had given her. Mr. Asquith could not fail to see his books on that favoured shelf the moment he came into the room.

He did not come into the room the next day, for Nancy was again away from home when he called. She had changed the hours of her music lessons at the Wilderness; she gave them in the afternoon now, and she did not get back to Cherry Garden until quite late, too late for anyone to call.

Augusta and Lucy saw through the flimsy *ruse* and were very angry with her.

"I think you are behaving very badly," her elder sister said severely, when Nancy came back flushed and smiling from the Wilderness, after Mr. Asquith had waited patiently for her for at least two hours, and had worn everybody's patience out in trying to entertain him.

Nancy turned to her sister a smiling face; she was standing before the glass taking off her hat, taking it off leisurely; she was never tired of seeing the face reflected in the glass, it always made her happy to see it, which is more than can be said of most reflections. Perhaps it will not always have the same effect.

The beautiful face in the glass was not only looking back to her to-day happy and smiling, it was looking more than happy—it was looking radiant. It flushed rosily as she smiled back at it, and her eyes seemed to darken and brighten.

"I think she is behaving shamefully!"

Lucy said in a little burst of anger and vexation; she had no patience with Nancy keeping that poor man in suspense so long, encouraging him, and drawing him on, as she had encouraged all the rest, playing with him as a cat would play with a mouse. "I expect she has been walking back with one of the masters, Mr. Earle or that German man; she wouldn't be so late if she hadn't been dawdling about the meadows with one of them. I daresay she's got one of them to propose; I believe she gets a man to propose to her every day, and she doesn't give any of them an answer; she keeps them all dangling after her. I'm quite ashamed of her!"

Poor Lucy! No one had ever proposed to her.

"You are wrong for once, Lu; it wasn't a schoolmaster to-day, dear. Gilbert Earle proposed yesterday, he couldn't propose again to-day," Nancy said gaily. She took off her hat as she spoke, and shook out her hair. It was beautiful, abundant brown hair, with a good deal of curl in it, and it fell over her face and hid her blushes—she was positively blushing.

Lucy saw the action, and she noted the unwonted colour, and the radiant happiness of the face in the glass, and her heart sank within her.

"It was not Mr. Earle," she said, "and it was not the German master, it—it——Oh! Nancy, it was not Mr. Craik!"

There was a cry of pain in her voice, and the colour dropped out of her cheeks.

"It does not matter to you who it was!" Nancy said sharply, still shaking the cloud of beautiful rich brown hair over her face, "it was none of your lovers, Lu. He wouldn't have proposed to you if there had not been another woman in the world!"

This was consoling, if not quite to the point.

"It *was* Mr. Craik!" Lucy said desperately. "Oh, Nancy, how horrid, how mean of you!"

Nancy laughed.

"You must blame Mr. Craik, you must not blame me; it is not my fault," she said, tossing back her hair for the pleasure of seeing it fall in rich waves upon her shoulders. "I can't help men running after me; there are hundreds of other girls in the world for them to run after, and they must take the consequences if they run after me. I can't marry them all. I should have to marry six at least, six or seven. I should have to set up as a female Bluebeard. I wonder which I should begin with. I think I should begin with a little one if I had to mince him up and pick his bones—a big one mightn't agree with me."

Lucy wouldn't hear another word of

such wicked frivolity; she fled from the room with her fingers in her ears to shut out the mocking voice and the laughter. She didn't quite shut it out when she got into her own room, which was opposite Nancy's, and had locked the door, and buried her face in the pillow, she could still hear Nancy laughing. She understood now why Douglas Craik had snubbed her in that unfeeling way when he had met her at Sarah Strong's.

Mr. Asquith made Nancy an offer the next day. He made it by letter.

He brought the letter himself the next day. It is not usual for Cupid to be his own postman—but except for the fact that he was in love, he did not very much resemble Cupid, unless Cupid had happened to be a trifle bald, and sallow, and wore glasses. Cupid, in the form of Mr. Asquith, was much muffled up about the throat on the occasion of delivering this missive; the wind had gone round to the East, and it had brought back a touch of his old bronchial complaint.

He really wanted a woman to nurse him, and coddle him up, and protect him from the east wind, and study his digestion, and take an interest in his pursuits.

He wanted a good unselfish woman who would have room enough in her kind heart to love him for his own true worth—gentle scholar, and true Christian gentleman as he was.

The world is full of good women ready enough to love a good man—and with this wealth of choice before him, Mr. Asquith had chosen Nancy Coulcher.

He had called at the time he had appointed the previous day, but finding Nancy out, he had left a letter. Augusta turned it over when he was gone; she was quite sure what it contained. She heard him cough as he went down the steps, after he had left it. She was sure by the way he coughed that he had made up his mind at last. She sighed and laid down the letter, and then she went to the window to look after him, to see that he had got his comforter on.

If he had only chosen Augusta!

Mr. Asquith's letter was like himself, dry and wordy, and to the purpose. He told Nancy in his prosy, considerate, old-fashioned way that his feelings for her had been gradually ripening into love, and that the discovery of their having so many tastes in common—tastes and pursuits, led him to hope for a favourable answer to his suit.

"What on earth does he mean by kindred pursuits?" Nancy said, holding the letter between her finger and thumb, and reading it at arm's length. "Oh, I know, he means the black beetles!"

"What will you do, dear?" Augusta

said softly. The sight of a love letter always moved her, she couldn't giggle over it like Nancy, and make fun of the writer. It seemed such a sacred thing, a man laying bare his heart to a girl, and offering her his best—his very best.

"Do?" repeated Nancy, with her eyes darkening, "do? why, refuse him of course. You don't think I'm going to marry that old stick!"

"Nancy!"

It quite took Augusta's breath away to hear her.

"You don't mean that you are going to refuse Mr. Asquith after—after all the encouragement you have given him?"

"Encouragement? I'm sure I haven't encouraged him. I didn't ask him to come here."

"But you led him on, Nancy; you knew exactly why he was coming. You made him believe every day that you liked him;

he would never have asked you to go over his house, and decide about his furniture, if he hadn't thought you were going to accept him."

"That's his mistake, not mine: I couldn't be rude to him when he came here bothering me about his things. You wouldn't have had me jump upon him!"

"I wouldn't have had you mislead a good, kind, considerate man, and persuade him that you cared for him, and then, when you had quite caught him, throw him over, and say you hadn't meant anything. I think it's shameful, Nancy, it's worse if anything than shameful, it's mean and base and horrid!"

Augusta was dreadfully in earnest.

Mr. Asquith had made a mistake—men generally do make mistakes. He had overlooked the one woman in the world who would have suited him exactly, who would have made him the best of wives, the most devoted of nurses, the intelligent companion of his studies, who would never have grown tired of pressing flowers, and who would have adored beetles.

CHAPTER VI.

NANCY'S LOVERS.

*" Stiles where we stay'd to be kind,
Meadows in which we met!"*

NANCY met Douglas Craik the next day as she came across the meadows.

The writing of that letter of dismissal to Mr. Asquith had not paled the roses on her cheeks or the light in her blue eyes. Douglas Craik thought he had never seen any eyes look so sweet as they looked to-day, as they smiled upon him, when he came up to her in the meadows.

They had never looked so blue before, so blue with a radiant quiver in them. There was a piteous pathetic smile on Nancy's face as she tried to speak to him, and she faltered and hung down her head with the words dying away on her lips.

It was really very prettily done.

"What is it, dear?" he said eagerly.

She did not speak, she only held out her hands to him. He caught them both in his and looked up into her sweet eyes.

"What is it?" he said huskily. "You don't mean——" he did not finish the question, he only stood holding her hands in his and looking into her eyes. He had a way of looking into people's eyes—his own eyes were so dark and earnest—that his poorer parishioners used to say that they looked as if he could see through them.

There was something besides earnestness in his dark eyes to-day, as he stood there looking through and through that shallow little Nancy. Perhaps he saw in her the ideal he had conjured up—his own ideal. Men generally do; they seldom see the real woman; the finer the nature the nobler the ideal.

"Yes," she said, answering his thought. "Mr. Asquith has proposed; he wrote to me last night."

"And you?" he said, holding her hand.

"I? I hate him! I wanted to tell him that I hated him, but mamma would insist on reading the letter. She is so angry with me for refusing him. They are all so angry. They say I am behaving shamefully because I have refused him! I couldn't do anything else. I couldn't marry one person caring for another—oh! what have I said!"

She was covered with confusion. The curate smiled; he appreciated the girlish simplicity of the avowal, and he pressed the little gloved hand he held tenderly; he had released one hand, but he still held the other, and he drew Nancy aside from the beaten path where any one might come across them at any moment, and led her down towards the river, beneath the high hawthorn hedge that was already white with blossom.

"You have said enough, dear, to make me very happy," he said softly, his heart was thumping so ridiculously that he could hardly get the words out—he had a heart a great many sizes too large for him. "You have said enough to give me courage to speak. Loving you as I do, I should not have dared to ask you to be a poor curate's wife, if you hadn't given me strength and courage. And you really, really have refused Mr. Asquith for my sake, Nancy?"

"Do you think I could have married *him*?" she said, with a very pretty shiver, "when I knew that—you—you——"

She didn't finish the sentence, but she looked down at him with her sweet eyes.

"That I loved you!" he added, filling up the gap with a gasp of happiness.

Douglas Craik would have liked to have gone down on his knees in the grass, under the hawthorn hedge, and thanked God for this great happiness. Nancy saw him looking up with his lips moving; she did not think Mr. Asquith would have thanked God if she had accepted him. He wanted to go back with her, he wanted to speak to her mother at once, but Nancy begged him to wait.

"They are all so angry at home, mamma and the girls, you must not say anything about it at present, Mr. Craik—Douglas. You must wait till this disappointment about Mr. Asquith has worn off. It would be no use to speak to mamma now. I will tell you when you may speak. You will be silent, dear, till I tell you?"

Douglas Craik was ready to promise anything. He was so full of his new, wonderful happiness that Nancy could have turned him round her finger. He promised her that he would tell no one of his engagement until he had her permission. He was quite satisfied. He had her promise.

"No one need know," she said, before she left him. "Let us keep this—this happiness to ourselves, Douglas."

"No one shall know," he answered.

* * * * *

Mr. Asquith had not accepted Nancy's refusal as final. He had written to her again; there was a letter awaiting her when she came back from that walk by the river with Douglas Craik. He had assured her of his devotion, and pleaded for an interview to explain the nature of his feelings.

The poor man felt that there must be a mistake—a great mistake; he couldn't understand a girl encouraging his attentions as Nancy had encouraged them, accepting his gifts, and going over his house planning his furniture, even to choosing the colour of the hangings, and—and refusing him.

There was some misapprehension, he was sure, that wanted explaining away.

Mrs. Coulcher was of the same opinion, she could not believe that Nancy would refuse such an eligible offer.

She followed Nancy into her bedroom, where she had flown up to, when she came in to read her letter. It was still open before her when her mother came into the room, and closed the door behind her.

"Have you thought about the answer you are going to give Mr. Asquith, Nancy?" she asked her daughter.

"I haven't any answer to give him, mother, but the answer I gave him yesterday. Nothing has happened to make me change my mind," Nancy said in her flippant way. She could never see things seriously.

"I don't think he understood that you had quite made up your mind, Nancy. You admitted in your answer, that you liked him—that you liked him and admired his great learning very much."

"Admiring his learning and his beetles has nothing to do with liking him as a husband. I only said I admired him because I thought it would be letting him down easily."

"Letting him down easily!"

Mrs. Coulcher was scandalized; she didn't know much of Nancy's little ways, perhaps she would not see more than she cared to see. She had a convenient way of shutting her eyes to things, and her ears too, if they happened to be unpleasant. It hadn't mattered very much while it was only the young masters at the grammar school and the curates. These were a shifting population; new masters were always coming and going, and the curates did not stay long in Stoke Edith; but this was the Rector's brother, the wealthy man of the neighbourhood. Nancy would not be likely to have such a chance as this again.

"Mr. Asquith couldn't expect me to love him, mamma," Nancy remonstrated in an injured voice, "he's twice as old as I am, and quite bald."

"Not *quite* bald, my dear."

"He's got a bald patch on the top of his head as big as — as the bottom of a tea-cup, and he stammers dreadfully, and he has always got a cold, or a cough, or something unpleasant."

"You knew all this before, Nancy," Mrs. Coulcher said severely. "Mr. Asquith has a great many admirable qualities that quite counterbalance these trifling defects, and he would give you a position in the county.

Ladylift is quite far enough away from the town to rank with the county. He would keep a brougham for you, and a landau —he was telling me about the landau yesterday; he has ordered it of one of the great London coachmakers, and he wanted to know what colour you would like to have the wheels painted."

"I hate landaus, they are so old-fashioned; I wouldn't have anything but a Victoria, but I'm not likely to have either, mamma," and then Nancy remembered Douglas Craik and his ridiculous income, and she sat on the edge of the bed and laughed.

"I'm sure Mr. Asquith would be delighted to give you a Victoria," Mrs. Coulcher said, eagerly following up her advantage. "He was asking me if you rode; he has been ordered by his doctor to take horse exercise, and he hoped you would ride with him. The horses are coming down to-morrow. There would be no harm in your riding with him if you were engaged. He told me about the horses a week ago, but I forgot to mention it to you."

"I don't think his horses or his carriages would make me alter my mind, mamma. They couldn't affect his stammer or the bald patch on the top of his head, or his liver. Oh! yes, they might shake up his liver; but I don't think they would make the hair grow on the top of his head."

Nancy ran on in her frivolous way.

It was no use reasoning with such an unreasonable girl, and Mrs. Coulcher left the room with a sigh. She was not without hope; but she knew enough of Nancy to feel that there was nothing to be gained by opposition.

Nancy sat down on the edge of the bed with a blotting book on her knees, and wrote her letter to Mr. Asquith when her mother was gone; it was rather a curt note, it positively refused an interview. She was not likely to change her mind, she told him. She was so full of those tender passages with Douglas Craik, beneath the hawthorn hedge, that she could say nothing less. She really meant, or thought she meant, what she said, which is much the same thing.

Lucy, who was always watching her, remarked her abstracted manner all through that long evening; it really seemed a long evening, for Nancy, who was generally the life of the party, was unusually silent.

She was thinking about Douglas Craik, and how he had looked into her eyes—into her soul—when he had asked her if she loved him, really, really loved him, better than anyone else in the whole world—he hadn't even mentioned Mr. Asquith, and how he had thanked God for the wonderful gift of her love. There seemed something like the reflection of his great happiness on Nancy's face as she sat at work, or pretending to work, in the long sweet Spring evening. Lucy watching her saw the smiles and the blushes, and the radiant light of a great happiness on Nancy's face, and she drew her own conclusions.

It was more than a suspicion that had crossed Lucy's mind, it was a certainty.

"Mr. Asquith has been here again this afternoon, Nancy," she said sweetly; "he was here more than an hour; mother couldn't get rid of him. He's been arranging about the carriages and horses; he's having a horse sent down for you to ride, a light chestnut. Do you like light chestnuts or bays best?"

Anyone would have thought that Nancy had accepted him to hear Lucy talk.

"I hate both, at least, I love both, only

I hate Mr. Asquith! I wish you wouldn't be continually harping upon him. I've told him I'm not going to marry him, and all the carriages and horses in the world won't make me alter my mind!"

Lucy smiled, she was used to Nancy's protestations.

"I wonder what he will do with the horse," Lucy went on, not heeding her sister's interruption. "He can't send it back, and Miss Asquith is too heavy and too old to ride. I wish he'd ask Augusta to ride it. She used to ride beautifully in Cornwall. Papa used to say she was a splendid horsewoman. She broke in the grey mare, you remember; no one could ride it till Augusta broke it in. I think mother might suggest it to Mr. Asquith. Her old habit would do very well with a little alteration."

Nancy's brow clouded.

"It would be a great liberty to suggest

anything of the kind," she said tartly. "It will be quite time enough for Augusta to alter her habit when Mr. Asquith asks her to ride the chestnut," and then she gathered up her work and went out of the room, banging the door after her in a most unladylike way.

Augusta was sitting with the boys in the schoolroom while Lucy had been talking; she generally sat with the boys in the evening, and helped them with their lessons. She had a class of little boys of her own by day that she was preparing for the grammar school, and she helped her brothers in the evening; her hands were always full. Mrs. Coulcher had gone into the drawing-room to write a letter to Mr. Asquith. She had fortunately intercepted Nancy's curt letter to her rejected lover, and she had put it discreetly into the fire. She excused Nancy's hasty rejection of his suit on account of her youth—her youth and her diffidence—she called it diffidence, and begged Mr. Asquith to give her time. His proposal had startled her by its suddenness—(she had been expecting it every day for a month past)—and she was too young and inexperienced to make up her mind. Mrs. Coulcher put it beautifully; no mother could have put it better. On the whole, it was very fortunate that she had stopped Nancy's letter in time.

The horses really came down the next day; a beautiful chestnut and a roan. Nancy met Mr. Asquith riding one, and the groom the other a few days later, when she was out with Augusta, and Mr. Asquith drew up at the curb to speak to her. He did not seem a bit hurt about the letter, she remarked; his manner was just the same as ever.

It had never occurred to her that he would stop his horse and speak to her, after—after what had passed. A sort of half-conscious, half-doubting look was in her eyes as he drew up; but she blushed and smiled; she did not attempt to run away. He really looked much better on horseback, she thought; the stoop in his shoulders did not matter so much, and he had left off his woollen comforter, and the exercise had brought some colour to his sallow cheeks.

Nancy had never seen him looking so well.

"I am so glad to meet you," he said when he came up. "I have called two or three times when you have been out; this is quite a happy chance."

"Oh, I am always out now in the afternoon," Nancy said blushing brightly; "I thought you knew; I have altered the time of my music lessons. What a lovely creature this is!"

She was patting the horse and fondling

him, as if she had been used to horses all her life, while Augusta, who was a splendid horsewoman, stood by glum and silent.

"This is the lady's horse," Mr. Asquith said, beckoning the groom to come up; "it is quite free from vice, and carries a lady splendidly."

The beautiful chestnut came up to the side of the path to be examined; and Nancy patted her, and admired her cleancut limbs, and her graceful shining neck. She would have given anything to be on its back flying over the country. She loved riding above everything. A ride on the back of this superb creature would have given her more pleasure, more real happiness, than anything else in the world. She only wanted to be happy, nothing more; she did not very much mind what her happiness cost others; that was their business, not hers.

"I wish you would try it some morning;

you have the mornings disengaged," Mr. Asquith was saying as she fondled the creature.

"I should like it immensely!" she said, lifting her radiant blue eyes to his, "only I haven't got a habit."

"You can wear mine," Augusta said sweetly.

"Oh, yours is old-fashioned and dowdy, and besides, it wouldn't fit me; it would be yards too short for me."

"I don't think that need matter," Mr. Asquith said promptly, and he mumbled something about "Lumby." Lumby was the tailor and habit maker of Stoke Edith.

"No, thanks, I must give it up," Nance said with a sigh, and she nodded to her rejected lover, and looked back regretfully after the shining steeds as they gallopped up the road into the beautiful green country.

She had forgotten all about the Curate of St. Radegund's.

She would have given anything to have been on the back of that chestnut flying across the country in the sweet May weather, instead of walking along the horrible dusty roads.

Mr. Asquith did not say anything about Nancy's rejection of his suit. He was quite willing to give her time. He would not have hurried her for the world. He knew nothing about girls. He had never asked a woman to marry him before, and he thought it was the way of the sex. He certainly preferred that a girl should take her time; should not decide in a hurry, jump down his throat, as it were. Nancy had not jumped down his throat. He could not understand her refusing him. He had always hitherto got everything he had made up his mind to in life; he could not understand being thwarted. Besides, he had settled to his own satisfaction that a great object lay before him in life, an object quite worth resigning his fellowship for—the moulding of the character of the girl he had decided to marry, and training her youthful mind in those abstruse studies that his soul delighted in.

CHAPTER VII.

"THAT FORWARD MINX!"

AUGUSTA COULCHER was not the only person in Stoke Edith who deplored Mr. Asquith's choice. The matter was discussed openly, at all the tea tables in Stoke; there was no secret made of it, and everybody had decided that it was a mistake, that the poor musty old college don was making a fool of himself.

His sister, who was ten years his senior, warned him in vain; he was deaf to her reasonings. Perhaps she was selfish, most maiden sisters are selfish on one point. They look with suspicion and dislike on any forward minx who may lie in waiting to snap up their unwary bachelor brothers.

Miss Asquith had kept house for her elder brother, the Rector of Stoke Edith, for twenty years, and no one had snapped him up yet. Perhaps the ladies of Stoke Edith had grown weary of trying. They let him alone now; they had let him alone for years, and the Rev. Cornelius was still a bachelor.

Not so his brother, the wealthy and learned Fellow of St. Catherine's; they had no intention of letting him alone.

There had been a flutter in the dovecotes of Stoke ever since his coming, the elderly dovecotes. The middle-aged spinsters of Stoke Edith, and some of the widows, had conceived a sudden surprising affection for Martha Asquith, and an interest in parish matters that ought to have delighted the heart of the rector. But the prosy middle-aged college don had not chosen one of these. He had chosen a ruddy, laughing, pert little minx, young enough to be his daughter.

"If it had only been the elder sister,

that nice girl, Augusta," Miss Asquith said to her friend and crony, Catherine Jayne, with a sigh.

"Lucy, you mean," said Miss Jayne sharply. "Lucy is worth a dozen of Augusta!"

"Lucy would have been better than—than the other," the rector's sister admitted, folding her fat hands meekly, and looking like a martyr—a well-fed martyr.

"I don't see how Augusta Coulcher could ever marry," Miss Jayne went on; she was very fond of arranging people's affairs for them. "I don't see what that poor woman could do without her, with all those boys, and such an invalid as she is. Augusta manages the whole household. She is an excellent girl in her way, but I prefer Lucy."

"Ye—es, either of them would be better than that forward minx. I never saw a girl give men so much encouragement in my life! I cannot think how Montagu can be so blind, so infatuated. The other day it was that young man at the grammar school, the man who left in a hurry, it was entirely on her account. I heard it from Cornelius, he is one of the governors. There would have been a scandal, but he hushed it up for the sake of the mother. Now she is flirting with another of the masters. I met them coming down the hill together the other day. You could hear them laughing the other side of the street, and he was carrying her fiddle! And then there is that poor curate——"

"What poor curate? You don't mean Craik?"

Miss Jayne sat quite upright on her chair, and pushed back her false curls, which had a habit of falling forward over her thin face, and her dark bright eyes seemed to grow darker and brighter.

"Of course I mean Craik—who else

should I mean?" Miss Asquith said in an injured voice. She hated to be tripped up, and Miss Jayne would never let her finish a story. She was always, she declared, ready to take the words out of her mouth.

Catherine Jayne was a sharp, keen-witted, rather flighty old lady, and the rector's sister was a fat, slow, ponderous old woman, who had always had her own way, and had ruled everybody about her as long as she could remember, and who hated to be contradicted.

"Oh, that's all nonsense! It's Lucy Coulcher, if it's anybody," Miss Jayne said in a superior way, with the manner of one who knew.

"It is not Lucy! She was here at a working party yesterday, and Mr. Craik didn't speak three words to her the whole time. And he let her walk back alone, though he was going her way, and she had a big bundle of work she would carry home with her to finish. He would have carried it fast enough if it had been Nancy!"

"Nancy — Nancy Coulcher! — " Miss Jayne repeated to herself; she had a habit of talking to herself even when people were present, as if she were thinking aloud. "He has never mentioned her name to me in his life, and he is always talking about Lucy. He would never be able to get through the work of the parish without Lucy. I thought — I hoped — perhaps some day——"

"Then you thought quite wrong."

"I am not so sure—I am not very often wrong—but I'll find out."

Miss Jayne got up and smoothed down her skirts, they always wanted smoothing down, as she wore a hoop; at least she wore a stiffener of some kind round the bottom of her gown. She still clung to the fashions of her youth. She smoothed down her dress, and drew on her lilac cotton gloves and went away.

"I shall not rest till I've found out," she said, as she went down the stairs.

The rector's sister watched her from the bow window of the rectory drawing room go down the street. She saw the top of her shabby green parasol—it had an ivory handle elaborately carved that had been brought from India—and the ridiculous purple flower nodding in her black bonnet, and her tall, spare figure, with the distended skirt, going briskly down the street.

"There will be mischief," she murmured to herself, as she stood watching the tall, upright, angular figure going down the street, with that air of purpose in every line of it. "I am sure there will be mischief!"

It really might have meant mischief, but the Curate happened to be ill.

He was so ill that his landlady—he lived over a music shop in the High Street—wouldn't let any one go up to see him.

"He's much too ill to see any one, ma'am," she said to Miss Jayne when she planted herself on the mat; "the doctor says he must keep quiet for two or three days, and he mustn't be worried about parish business."

"I should think not," said Miss Jayne stoutly, "you are quite right to keep the people off, and I'm sure those pianos in the shop ought not to be going; he can't be kept quiet, with all that Babel in his ears!"

She did not stop to listen to the woman's indignant protest; she brushed by her and went up the stairs to the Curate's room.

He really was ill. He had been overdoing himself and he had broken down. He could not do things reasonably like other men; he could not keep back anything: health or strength, or time or money. Whatever he had he gave: he kept nothing back.

He was not content to preach two sermons in the church on Sundays, but he must go out into the market place, and hold an open-air meeting when the evening service was over. It was all very well to speak in the church, where the walls and the roof gave back the sound, but to go out into the open air, to stand bare-headed in that draughty market place, shouting himself hoarse for an hour, when he was already worn out and exhausted, was another thing. It brought on a touch of his old lung trouble, and he was confined to the house for a week, and the doctor forbade any more open-air meetings.

It did not seem, to look at him as he sat coughing in that bare, chilly room on that chilly Spring day, that he would hold many more meetings, outdoor or indoor. There was a suspicious hectic colour on his thin cheeks, and his cough was troublesome. Miss Jayne had never remarked how thin and hollow his cheeks were until she saw him sitting there in that uncomfortable leather armchair, with the light from the two windows falling upon him.

He didn't half fill up the big, roomy leather chair—it would have taken an alderman to fill it up—and there were no cushions in it to help him out, to fit into the hollows. His face looked paler and thinner against the high leather back than she had ever seen it look before, and his shoulders were limp and stooping.

His rooms had a bleak aspect, they were on the wrong side of the road for an invalid.

It was very uncertain May weather, warm one day and cold the other, with a nip of east wind in it. There was a nip of east wind in it to-day, in spite of the sunshine. The Curate's landlady had got her spring cleaning over too early; and she had been in too great a hurry to put up the lace curtains. The flimsy bit of white muslin that hung up before the two draughty, ill-fitting windows, let in the cold wind, and there was no sunshine that side of the street to warm it. The room was chilly and draughty, and there was only a mere handful of fire in the grate.

"Oh, dear, this will never do," Catherine Jayne said, bustling about the bare, comfortless room, trying the window catches, and drawing over the ridiculous lace curtains; "with that cough you ought to be in bed; you ought not to be sitting in this draught, and what a poor fire!"

She attacked the coal-scuttle, a deceiving, ornamental, lodging-house affair, with a lid that concealed its nakedness, but it was empty.

"Oh, this is very careless of Mrs. Bolt,

she ought to see that you had plenty of firing," she said indignantly. "Why do you let her neglect you like this? Why don't you ring the bell and have some coals brought up?"

Then the Curate had to explain, and the explanation brought on the cough.

"It's my fault," he stammered, or rather coughed. "I—I don't feel I can afford it. Coals cost so much, a shilling a scuttleful I pay for them; it is fairer to pay by the scuttle, and then I only pay for what I use, and there is so much better use I can make of a shilling than wasting it on coals."

Miss Catherine Jayne sniffed; she had an aggressive way of sniffing that meant volumes—and she rang the bell.

"Will you bring up some coals?" she said to the servant who appeared, "a scuttle of coals—a full scuttle. I never heard such a thing," she said indignantly, "as a shilling a scuttle for coals, and in May, too! If they cost a guinea a scuttle you must have them; I'm sure I don't know what better use you can make of your money than to buy necessaries. I know exactly what you do; you can't deceive me, Mr. Craik, you deny yourself everything that you may spend your money upon the people in the parish. Don't tell me you don't—I've seen it with my own eyes. I went into Mary Love's cottage, the other day when she was at dinner—I generally drop in when the people are at dinner or at tea, or when they don't expect me—and she had a boiled chicken on the table—a boiled chicken in May! When I asked her where it came from, she told me that you had sent it—as if you didn't want boiled chickens yourself as much as Mary Love, who has the pay of the parish! And old Silas Hancock had a bottle of port wine hidden away in the cupboard behind his bed, that you had sent him. He couldn't hide it away from me. I always look in that cupboard when I go to see him, and I made him tell me where it came from. I have no patience with you giving away all your money, and denying yourself common necessaries."

The Curate's pale face flushed.

"Mary Love has a daughter dying of consumption," he said gravely; "she will not require boiled chickens long, and poor old Hancock cannot turn in bed. It is very little I can do, and there is so much to be done. I cannot visit people and see their need of help—a little help goes a long way with the poor—without doing something for them, not much. You forget I am only an Almoner."

Miss Jayne did not ask him whose Almoner; she blew her nose rather vigorously and stirred up the unwilling embers in the grate, dropping in with extreme caution some lumps of coal from the box the girl had just brought up.

"Do you call this full?" she said to the servant, pointing indignantly to the open box.

"It's as much as I could carry, mum," the girl said sulkily; "it's a lot of stairs to carry it up, and Mr. Craik said I wasn't to overfill it; I oughtn't to carry so much."

"I've really no patience with you," the old lady said, when the girl had gone, "encouraging people to rob you! You want some one to look after you; you are not fit to take care of yourself. You ought to have a sister or a wife——"

She paused when she spoke of a wife and remembered her errand. She had forgotten it until now.

"A wife," he said with a smile, and his lips quivering, and a lovely pink flush spreading over his delicate face, "a wife! I am not likely to be in a position to keep a wife for years. What girl would marry a curate with a hundred and fifty pounds a year?"

"No one but a fool would!" Miss Jayne said with great decision, "and only a very foolish young man—a very wicked, selfish young man—would ask a girl to share such a lot. What isn't enough for one, can never, by the greatest economy, be made enough for two; and girls of the present day are not economical; they think of nothing but their clothes and their amusements, and when a family comes — and the poorer the household the larger the family — there is nothing but destitution before them. They will wake up too late to find the old adage true, that 'when poverty comes in at the door it drives love out of the window.'"

The Curate sighed.

"Yes," he said sadly, with all the beautiful pink dying out of his face, and his lip quivering, " a curate who has no means of his own, has no right to marry. He has no right to drag a girl down with him."

There was nothing more said about marrying—about marrying and courting. Douglas Craik was much too conscientious to ask a girl to share his poverty, too honourable to ask a girl to lose all her best days waiting for him, he had as good as said so. Miss Catherine Jayne went away satisfied, or almost satisfied. Her protegé, who denied himself a scuttle of coals, would not be likely to think of marriage. No, Martha Asquith's suspicions were unfounded. She was jealous, quite naturally jealous of "the minx" who had beguiled her brother.

Before she went away Miss Jayne had an interview with the landlady below stairs. She asked if there was any soup or beef-tea preparing for the curate's dinner.

There was not any soup, but there was a mutton chop.

A mutton chop she learned was an unusual delicacy. Mr. Craik did not often indulge in a mutton chop; he did not often indulge in meat at all. He had a light lunch, a very light lunch, and a late meat tea, when the work of the day was over.

Miss Jayne, who had a habit of finding out things, of getting at the bottom of them, as she used to express it, ascertained before she went away that the curate's late meat tea usually took the form of a bloater or a kidney, or some such nutritive delicacy as anchovy paste, or sardines.

It was all over the parish the next day that Douglas Craik was starving himself, that he was being robbed through thick and thin by his landlady, and that the *pièce de résistance* of his frugal meal was a red herring.

CHAPTER VIII.

"TUM-TUM-TE-TUMTY."

But the stalwart old woman who acted the part of Providence at Stoke Edith did not stop with reports. She could not help telling people how badly the curate was served, and what a fool he made of himself. Miss Jayne never minced matters—she always spoke her mind, but she told them also what a self-denying life he was leading, how he was acting up to his profession. He was not standing up in the pulpit preaching one thing and in his everyday life doing another. However strict the rule he preached to others, he was practising it himself, to the very letter.

Somehow the little white-faced curate was a favourite at Stoke. People believed in him. It does not take much to make people believe in the real thing when they happen to get it. There is no mistaking it. It has the true ring. His little earnest sermons went straight to the heart of the congregation of St. Radegund's. They were not learned or scholarly discourses like the sermons of the Rev. Cornelius, but they went straight to the hearts of the people. When they were sick or dying they sent for the curate, and he helped them through their trouble. It was a comfort they used to say, a stay in the time of extremity, to have someone near who believed in what he taught, whose bodily presence, however weak, was as a strong tower in the face of the enemy.

There were a lot of old women at Stoke, wealthy widows and well-endowed spinsters who had profited by Douglas Craik's ministrations. He used to drink tea with one or the other of them nearly every day in the week—little gossippy afternoon teas, but their generosity, or hospitality rather, had never gone beyond this.

It went beyond it after that visit of Catherine Jayne's. It was astonishing how many old women suddenly remembered that the Curate wanted beef-tea and hot-house grapes, and rich soups, and that carriage drives would be beneficial to him. Several of the old ladies sent him nicely-worded notes with a crisp enclosure that rustled delightfully when he opened them, begging him to devote them—the crisp enclosures—to carriage drives—and to getting well.

He devoted the first of these enclosures to a present for Nancy, a gold bangle with a heart attached to it—his own heart—and he clasped it round her white arm with his trembling hands. He could not keep them from trembling; he was weak still from his illness when he met her at the stile on that first evening when he was well enough to get out, and that near contact with her sent thrills of inexpressible tenderness through him.

"You will wear it for my sake, darling," he said, "it will remind you of your promise. It will be a long time before I am able to claim it, Nancy, it will be years and years, perhaps, but you will wait for me?"

There was just a suspicious catch in his voice when he asked Nancy if she would wait for him. He would not have had her remark it for the world, it was as if he were doubting her.

"Of course I'll wait for you!" she said sweetly, and then she went into raptures with the bracelet.

It was not the only gold bracelet she had with a heart attached to it. The master at the grammar school, the young classical master who had gone to India, had given her a gold bracelet with a heart attached to it before he went away.

There was a key attached to the heart, and he had locked it on her arm, and she had promised to wear it till he came back, —and she had promised to wait for him. He wrote to her by every mail; she had got a letter from him only that morning, but she had broken the lock of that ridiculous heart long ago; she could not break the lock without breaking the heart, and she had tossed it into a drawer with her trinkets and laces.

The other enclosures Douglas Craik really had applied to the purposes for which they were sent. He had taken carriage drives daily, he had taken the opportunity of visiting all his neglected outlying parishioners that he could not very well get at on foot. He had not gone alone; he had taken all the old men who lived in the alms houses just outside the town, out with him, a carriage full at a time, in his daily drives. He had picked them up and dropped them down at their own doors before he came into the town, so that no one was any the wiser. The circle of blessing described by those crisp five-pound notes had widened considerably beyond the intention of their donors—perhaps it is widening still.

The daily drives, or the soup, or the beef-tea, or the rest, and giving up those open-air meetings, worked miracles. Perhaps it was the Spring weather; it had really come in warm, and a south wind was blowing. Something had brought a faint flush of colour back into Douglas Craik's thin cheeks and his cough was better. It was so much better that he was able to preach a few Sundays later, and when he stood up again in the pulpit after his illness there was nothing to tell of it but a little preliminary huskiness which wore off as he warmed into his sermon.

Some people remarked, looking up to him there, with his face outlined against the grey stone wall of the church, that a change had come over him since that last attack. His eyes were brighter, they were very bright dark eyes, and they looked darker against the whiteness of his face. It was a smooth, white face, like a girl's; it looked chiselled in marble, only that there was a quiver about the lips, that no marble ever had, and that no one had remarked before.

It was the face of a man who could do noble things: it might be the face of a saint.

The story of those five-pound notes had got whispered about the parish—everything gets whispered about a gossipping country town. Lucy had heard of it among the rest; Miss Catherine Jayne had told her; she was a favourite of Miss Catherine's, and she told her about her visit to the curate in his illness, and the shower of five-pound notes that had been the result of it.

"He is as poor as a church mouse, my dear," she had told Lucy. Perhaps she had her own reasons for telling her: "he hadn't got a spark of fire in the grate, and he was afraid to ring the bell for coals, and that woman is robbing him shamefully! He ought to have a wife to look after him; he is not fit to look after himself, but how can he ever marry on such an income? He has no private means; a man without private means has no right to go into the Church. The Church is supported by the clergy now-a-days, not the clergy by the Church. Talk of disestablishment, what would the Church do without their aid?"

Lucy murmured a faint approval; she didn't care much about disestablishment; curates couldn't be worse paid if the

Church were disestablished to-morrow—they couldn't get less pay or harder work.

"A man ought to have money or influence to go into the Church," Miss Catherine continued, laying down the law as if she were Archbishop of Canterbury, "and that poor young man has neither. He is never likely to get a living above two hundred a year, and it would be nothing short of madness to marry upon that. What is two hundred a year to keep a wife upon—a wife and family?—there would be sure to be a family—a dozen children perhaps—curates always have large families; their quivers are always over-full, and very likely an ailing wife—a woman cannot go on having children without her health giving way—and he such a poor fellow and wanting so much nursing."

Lucy repeated this conversation when she went back to Cherry Garden. She repeated it when Nancy was present.

Nancy was making herself a summer frock; the Coulcher girls made their own frocks. Somehow, whatever might be the state of the family finances, Nancy managed to get new frocks. It was a pink frock she was making, and it matched her complexion, and made it look more brilliant than ever. She was trying it on before the glass, when Lucy was pouring out the dismal tale of the curate's fireless grate, and the empty coal scuttle, and being afraid to ring the bell, and the five-pound notes that the rich old women had sent to him, and the beef-tea and the soup.

Lucy kept nothing back.

Nancy was wearing the gold bracelet with the pendant heart that Douglas Craik had locked upon her arm, and of which he had kept the key. There were no sleeves to the pink frock yet, it was being tried on a bit at a time, and the gold bracelet was gleaming on Nancy's bare arm. She was admiring it in the glass, while Lucy was talking—the gleam of the gold against the fine smooth whiteness of her skin. It was a lovely, plump, rounded arm. Lucy could not help thinking of old Sarah Strong's brown, wrinkled, skinny wrist, the wrist that had clung to her with such terrible tenacity, as she saw the beautiful, white, rounded thing wreathing backwards and forwards in the arrangement of the puffs and plaits of that pink body, and the gold bracelet slipping up and down.

"Where did you get that bracelet from, Nancy?" she asked suddenly.

"Oh, I've had it a long time."

"You can't have had it long; it's quite a new one. Did Mr. Asquith give it to you?"

"Mr. Asquith! I should think not. It's my old one. I've had it for months!"

"The one Gervase Scott gave you?"

Nancy nodded, and laughed. She could

tell tarradiddles by the yard without a change of countenance.

Lucy didn't believe her, she had a vision of that discarded gold bracelet lying somewhere upstairs in a drawer, among a litter of ribbons and laces.

"Miss Jayne is dreadfully distressed about that poor Mr. Craik," Lucy went on a little spitefully. "She thinks he ought to marry a wealthy woman, he wants such a lot of nursing and nourishing things. He will never be able to marry a girl without money; he hasn't got a penny in the world, and no influence; he can't get a living worth having without some money, without influence. Think what a life it would be for any poor girl who was foolish enough to marry him, with nothing to look forward to but poverty and debts, and a dozen children and a sick husband——"

"Did she say a dozen children?" Nancy

asked from before the looking-glass. "Are you *sure* you haven't made a mistake in the number?"

"It doesn't matter whether it was six or a dozen!" Lucy said impatiently. "It comes to the same thing; whoever marries the poor man will make a dreadful mistake —she will ruin his life as well as her own!"

"Six children can never be the same as a dozen," Nancy said flippantly, "it's a serious difference. She must have made a mistake somewhere. I wonder where she got the number from, the exact number—I shall ask her when I see her. Could Mr. Craik have told her?"

Despite her flippancy, Nancy Coulcher was moved with the picture Lucy had drawn of the Curate's wife. Twelve children, and a sick husband, and a poor home—the picture was too dreadful!

How could Miss Jayne have conjured up

such a picture? She should have stopped with the empty coal scuttle and the five pound notes.

What would he do when the five-pound notes ceased? They would cease directly he married, and the beef tea and the grapes, and the slippers and all the knitted things would cease too. There would be no more gold bracelets.

Nancy threw off the pink frock impatiently—all the charm had gone out of it. It didn't suit her at all. It was a horrid shade of pink; she couldn't think how she could have chosen it! Pink was a mistake after all; blue suited her complexion best, blue that matched her eyes and provoked comparisons.

She flung the pink frock down of a heap on the chair and bounced out of the rooms and the girls sitting at work at the open window, heard her playing a jig on her fiddle in the room below.

Tum-tum-te-tumty!

It was a hateful tune, it set their teeth on edge as they listened to it, and Lucy got up and shut the window with a bang. Nancy heard her shut it, and she played a little louder.

Tum-tum-te-tumty!

"Has she got any heart?" Lucy asked angrily — she could not help being angry. Old Miss Jayne's account of the Curate's poverty and weakness, and the dreary future that lay before him, had moved her to tears, but it had only provoked Nancy to laughter — laughter and mockery.

"Yes, I think she has sometimes," Augusta said slowly, holding her work before her eyes that she might see the set of it, "but it will not make any difference —it will not prevent her marrying Mr. Asquith."

"You think she will marry him after

all?" Lucy gasped. "She told me she had quite given him up!"

"Yes, she has given him up, but she will marry him nevertheless."

And meanwhile Nancy was playing her jig in the room below.

Tum-tum-te-tumty!

CHAPTER IX.

"DOUGLAS, DOUGLAS, TENDER AND TRUE."

Douglas Craik had never been in love before. It was his first, his very first love, a sacred flame, burning on a pure altar.

There was something infinitely touching and tender in his love for Nancy Coulcher; there was nothing earthy or gross in it—it was scarcely material—it was a devotion, a consecration, a surrender, all the more complete because it was unconscious and beyond his control. He could not have helped loving her if he would.

He went about his daily duties after that happy morning, like one in a dream—a beautiful dream. He asked himself a hundred times a day if it were true. He could not understand how Nancy could love him, what she could have seen in him to love, to give up Mr. Asquith — Mr. Asquith was his rector's brother—with his horses and carriages, and his position in the county, and be willing to marry him, a poor Curate, with a hundred and fifty pounds a year!

It was past understanding. He could only accept this great gift as from the hand of the Great Giver. He accepted it it humbly, thankfully; he thanked God for it every day—a thousand times a day —and he kept silence.

He did not breathe a word to anyone of his engagement; he was content to trust Nancy, and believe in her, and see her whenever she would let him. She would not let him walk back with her from the Wilderness now so often as before her engagement. She had begun to be careful and think what people would say; she was quite sure everybody would be talking about her if Douglas Craik were seen with her so often. He submitted with a sigh and consoled himself by writing letters to her daily. The postman used to come to Cherry Garden at an unearthly early hour, as it happened to be beyond the town delivery and was on the round of the country postman, who started at daybreak. Nancy used to slip downstairs noiselessly when she heard him coming up the steps, and secure her treasure and come back to bed to devour it.

They were lovely letters, unlike any love letters she had ever received before, and she had received a good many. They kept her awake at first, and sometimes she would read them twice over—they were closely written, and covered an enormous number of pages, which was quite a test of the depth of his affection. It was wonderful what Douglas Craik could find to say in so many words and to cover so much paper.

Nothing ever happened at Stoke Edith, and there is so little really to be said, when one comes to think of it. It is quite astonishing in what a few sentences one can sum up the longest love letter. It is all variations of the same air; the verb *aimer* conjugated *ad infinitum*.

Is anything more needed?

Then had come his illness when his letters were twice their usual length; he had no sermons to write, so that he could spend all his time writing to Nancy. He had said nothing about the five-pound notes in his letters, only that the people had been very, very, very good to him. They had shown him a thousand times more kindness than he deserved. They had loaded him with gifts, beef tea, port wine, soup, grapes; he was surrounded with luxuries. At least a dozen knitted comforters had come in, and his room was quite a bower of hot-house flowers. Nancy had called at his lodgings and left a bunch of flowers for him once: she had called from her mother to make enquiries. It was only a bunch of pinks and double stocks and sweet briar she had snatched up as she passed through the garden; it was quite an afterthought to gather them, and she hadn't even tied them together. He had put the white pinks and double stocks in water, and kept them by his side until they tumbled to pieces, and he had pressed the sweet briar between the leaves of his sermons.

The least he could do after so much attention being shown him by the parish, was to get well again. He got well without delay. He was in such a hurry to get well. He was dying to see Nancy again; he could not see her in his bachelor rooms, his only chance was to get well. The first time he saw her after his illness, he had clasped that gold bracelet round her arm. If he had told her that he had bought it with the money that was sent to him to spend in getting well, in taking daily drives, she might not have accepted it, so he held his tongue.

He had hesitated to talk about those five-pound notes. He did not like to tell Nancy that he had been an object of charity. He had accepted them with some hesitation, but he had not been humiliated in accepting them, but with Nancy it might be different; she might take it as a humiliation, accepting gifts of money. The time had gone on and he had not spoken about the money, and it was hard to speak now. Perhaps she would think, if she heard of it, that if he wanted help now, money help, when he had only himself to keep, when there was no one dependent upon him, that he would want it more by-and-bye, when there was a wife—and children—that he would have to go round with a bag. He was a dreadful coward when it came to raising obstacles in the way of his love for Nancy, and he was afraid the money would be an obstacle. He surprised Nancy just outside the Wilderness gate, one afternoon a week after that casual meeting with Mr. Asquith by the roadside. Nancy knew exactly why he had come; it was not one of the days he was allowed to meet her, and he had said nothing about it in his morning's letter. She saw by the cloud on his brow as she came to him across the grass, that there was something amiss.

At the sight of the radiant vision coming towards him in the sunshine, the cloud ought to have disappeared. Nancy greeted her lover as she greeted all her admirers, with her brightest smile; she made no difference.

"You here!" she said in a tone of

surprise, as if he were the last person in the world she expected to meet.

"Yes!" he answered rather huskily, his face unconsciously relaxing under her smiles, and the cloud melting away—it could not stay there long with her smiling upon him, " yes, darling, I could not keep away! I—I wanted to ask you something —something I have heard—if it were true, that—that you had gone out riding this morning with Mr. Asquith?"

He couldn't ask the question quite steadily; he couldn't keep a tremor out of his voice.

"Lucy has told you this?" she said turning upon him with a sudden anger in her eyes, and the crimson colour leaping into her face. It was quite a new thing to see her angry, it was new and becoming.

"Yes," he said, "I met your sister at Sarah Strong's, and I asked after you, and she told me you were riding with Mr.

Asquith. Why should she not tell me? Is it a secret?"

Something in his voice recalled her to herself, and she laughed her little gay laugh.

"Secret? Of course it's no secret, only I hate people to talk about me. Mr. Asquith asked me to try his new horse, and I rode with him for an hour this morning. There was no harm in my riding with him; Augusta would have gone, but her habit was so shabby. Lumby offered to lend me a habit that exactly fitted me; they hadn't got one to fit Augusta."

He was not listening to the story about the habit, he was looking into the girl's eyes in that direct way he had, as if he would read her heart.

"No," he said with a sigh, "there is no harm in your riding with Mr. Asquith, I suppose, only—only——"

He broke off lamely, and looked at the girl with a question, a half doubt in his eyes.

"Only what?" she interrupted gaily.

"After what has passed, after your having so recently rejected him, I did not think you would care to ride with him," he said awkwardly. He knew he was making a brute of himself; he was ashamed of himself for doubting her for a moment.

Nancy laughed.

"Oh, that is all over," she said sweetly, "he has accepted his dismissal; the dear old thing did not say a single word about it. We talked of nothing but the horses, and the country; the country was looking lovely! I enjoyed it so much, I don't know when I've enjoyed anything so much. I love riding better than anything in the world!"

The Curate of St. Radegund's sighed.

He was thinking Nancy would not get much riding as a Curate's wife; he would give her his best—his very best—but it would never be likely to run to a horse. The most he could ever hope to be able to give her, would be a pony carriage, or a "tub," and a quiet, sure-footed old pony. Nancy was giving up a great deal for him, a wealthy suitor, and a position in the county, and the pleasure she loved better than anything else in the world!

He could not be hard upon her when he remembered what she was giving up for him.

"When may I speak to your mother, Nancy?" he asked her before they parted, when the cloud had quite dispersed, and he had told himself that he was unreasonably jealous, and was heartily ashamed of himself for his doubts and suspicions. "I am sick of this suspense and secrecy, I want to have the right to come openly. What is there to wait for?"

"Not yet, Douglas, not yet; you would have no chance with mamma yet. She has not forgiven me about Mr. Asquith. You must give her time to get over it. I will tell you when to speak, dear. You can trust me, Douglas?"

Trust her—how could he help trusting her, looking down at him with her beautiful smile, and a tear, just a suspicion of a tear, in her beautiful eyes? How could he wrong her with his base unworthy suspicions?

They were no longer in the meadows now, they had wandered off into the lane, and the hedges, the sweet hawthorn hedges rose high on either side. There was not a soul in sight, there would not be likely to be a soul in sight in that unfrequented lane, at that time in the day. There were no jealous eyes watching them, only the darling speedwell's innocent blue eyes staring straight up into Heaven. Douglas Craik took her in his arms, he could do nothing else, and vowed he would never doubt her again, never, never. Nancy was moved in spite of herself by his devotion; her eyes were wet with real tears as her face drooped on to his shoulder with a sudden strange emotion that was quite new to her.

This was really love; something she had never felt before, and for a moment, while her head rested on Douglas Craik's shoulder, Nancy felt she wouldn't have married Mr. Asquith for the world; that it was all quite settled now, that there were no more doubts, or bewilderment, or uncertainty. Fate had chosen for her, and it was all settled beyond recall. She had drifted into a calm haven, with her lover's arms around her, and his kisses on her lips, and his dear voice in her ears; she had drifted into a peaceful harbour: she was so safe, so secure in his love; she could not keep her tears from falling, and her lips were tremulous and tender.

"You must never doubt me again, Douglas," she murmured, "I love you better than anyone in the world! I hate Mr. Asquith and his horses and things; Oh! if you only knew how I hate him. I would rather live in a cottage with you, Douglas—why shouldn't we live in a cottage, a dear little rosey, bowery, cottage? I'm sure I would rather live in a dear little cottage than a big house with a lot of tiresome servants. I would rather marry you, darling, and live in a tiny wee cottage, than marry Mr. Asquith with his great house and his carriages and horses."

She said it very prettily, and she really thought she meant it.

Douglas Craik assured her that he would never be jealous again, that, whatever happened, he would trust her; how could he help trusting her after that outspoken confession?

They walked back by the river; it was a long way round, but they had nothing to hurry for. The afternoon sun was shining, and the river was flashing in the sunlight, and from the meadows came the fresh, sweet smell of the new-mown hay; the blue forget-me-nots in the bank were crowding up at their feet, and the lonely yellow iris out in the stream, was unfolding its inmost heart to the sun. A green, glowing valley spread out before them, and above an intense heaven was melting into light.

They walked back to Stoke Edith in a golden beatitude; the air was full of sweet scents and mysterious tones; there was not a single cloud on the horizon; a change had come over the whole world.

"I suppose he will have to ask mamma soon," Nancy said to herself as she turned the corner of Cherry Garden alone. "Of course I shall marry him. I don't mind the dear little cottage a bit. I have never, never loved any of the rest half so much. Douglas, Douglas, tender and true!"

She really meant it this time. She was prepared for the sacrifice. This was before she had heard that story of the five-pound notes—and the twelve children.

CHAPTER X.

SARAH STRONG.

The Curate of St. Radegund's got well as suddenly as he had fallen ill. He looked quite a new man after that illness, if ever he could be said to look like a man at all. His face was too white and clean-shaven and delicate for a man's; it was much more like a girl's face. The face of a beautiful woman who had suffered, who had gone through trial and anguish, and vicarious suffering, and who had come out of it purified, with increased capacities for self-denial, and sacrifice if need be.

At least, so it looked to the admiring female members of the congregation of St. Radegund's. The male portion took a different view—they generally do—they thought he was a poor washed-out kind of fellow, with no back-bone, only fit to be petted and made much of by silly women. He was a woman's curate, they said good-naturedly, not a man's curate.

Perhaps he recognised his weakness himself. He had done good work in a crowded London parish, but he was not doing much work here. There were no temptations there in that London slum to draw him away from his work; there was nothing to keep him from throwing himself, heart and soul, into it.

But here—here there was a siren with drooping eyelids and a bewitching smile, who was always using her wiles to draw him away from his work, whose lovely image was never out of his mind.

Douglas Craik could hardly believe his happiness. To find himself with his heart's desire, the full, rich fruition of his hopes, within his grasp, was more than he could understand. The bliss was so keen it was almost akin to pain. To wake up in the morning and tell himself that Nancy loved him, that she had passed by all the rest, and chosen—*him*—seemed like a dream, a beautiful dream; he could hardly believe he was waking! He tried very hard not to let his happiness—his great happiness he called it—interfere with his work, but he could not keep it out of it. It came between him and his duty a thousand times a day. When he was reading the morning lesson—they had daily prayers at St. Radegund's—the beautiful face of his betrothed would come between him and the words he was reading, and he would lose his place, and forget where he had left off. He had, besides the daily service at the church, and the meetings, a good deal of visiting to do in the parish; the Rector never by any chance "visited," so the Curate's hands were always full. He used to map out a certain number of old men and women and sick folk to see every day, and take the list up to the rectory at the end of that week. He was startled in adding up the list of his visits at the end of that week of Elysium, to find that he had fallen short of his usual number.

His happiness, in fact, had been all his own, no one else had benefited by it. Happiness isn't much good if it doesn't benefit other people. Love ought to have been an inspiration, but it had only made him selfish and neglect his duty.

A man with such a face as Douglas Craik, with his experience, his lofty ideal, and his little white soul, ought not to have been drawn away from his duty by a shallow, frivolous creature, with no other recommendation than a trick of smiling.

If it had been a good woman who had drawn him away, it would have been different; but a good woman would not have drawn him away from his work. She would have stimulated him to higher effort. Perhaps this is a test, a crucial test of the lower and the higher natures; the lower nature that enervates and drags down; the high strain that ennobles and stimulates to effort and work.

It was the old story of St. Anthony and his temptation. It was certainly not a saint that tempted the good St. Anthony. He is still represented in Anglican art, attended by swine. It is his symbol, and has its own significance. He has been known by it through all the ages, as other saints and holy men of old have been known by the emblems of their sufferings and temptation and victory.

Douglas Craik did not take the list of his visits over to the rectory, as he was accustomed to do, on that Saturday afternoon. He usually went over early, directly after lunch, and talked over parish matters with his rector, going through the list of the sick and needy parishioners he had visited during the week, and explaining the notes he had made against their names. There was generally a good deal to explain. Although the Rector did not visit himself, he was careful to see that his flock was well looked after, that they did not suffer from his neglect. If he did not minister to the spiritual wants of his poor people, he was not backward in the matter of necks of mutton when they were needed, or port wine, or grapes; his purse and his cellar and his greenhouse were open to the sick of the parish all the year round. Every one allowed that he might have done more for the parish, but he certainly might have done less.

Douglas Craik didn't see how he could spare time to go over to the rectory that Saturday afternoon; there were no urgent cases in need of grapes and port wine, and the necks of mutton could stand over. He had lost enough time this week dreaming about his own wonderful happiness, he could not afford to lose any more. He could get in, he told himself, three, perhaps four visits this afternoon, if he looked sharp about it.

He got in more than four—looking sharp about it—and he found he had just time to get in another visit before tea. He hadn't seen Sarah Strong since the day when Lucy had told him that her sister was riding with Mr. Asquith. He generally met Lucy there; the old woman was in her district, and the more cantankerous and disagreeable she grew, the more frequently Lucy Coulcher visited her. The poor old soul was failing fast; it did not seem likely that she would be cantankerous much longer. She would lose this infirmity with the rest, with the rheumatism, and the pains, and the sleepless nights. She wouldn't groan, or complain, or bully people much longer—it was the only satisfaction that was left to her in life, to grumble and find fault with everybody.

She was finding fault with Lucy when the Curate went in.

Lucy had been trying to show her that she had had a great many things to be grateful for in life, but the old woman had refused to see it. She had been poor all her life, and had had to work hard—to toil from morning till night—to live on the hardest and scantiest fare. She had known grievous trouble, a drunken husband, and an idiot daughter; the rest of her children were dead or had gone away; they had died to her years ago. She had none left —everyone belonging to her was gone— she was left in her old age and her weakness to suffer and complain alone. She refused to see in the long sad history of her dreary past, the hand of a kind Providence leading her by dark and difficult ways to the peace and the rest beyond. The future was as dark to her as the past; it only meant for her oblivion and rest. She didn't trouble herself about judgment to come. Perhaps in her heart she did not believe that a God, who was always represented to her as a God of Love, would visit on a poor old creature, whose life had been one long tale of suffering from beginning to end, eternal torments and agonies. She had some sense of justice—the poor always have, and if she did not believe in the love of God, she had a blind, dim faith in His justice. In her ignorant, groping way she believed, somehow, that the God she had worshipped all these years was not small-minded, and would not wrong the least and meanest of his creatures.

"I've had my turn already," she was saying to Lucy when the Curate went in.

"I've gone through more'n most folks in my time, an' I've come to the end. I'm past bearin' more if the Lord puts it upon me. I can't believe that He will—a poor, broken old soul, worn out wi' her groanin's. He's tooked from me all there was to take—husband, and children—there's none left. I can't think why He left me lyin' here, and they that were young and strong should be took."

Then Lucy tried to explain, but the old woman would not hear; perhaps it was quite as well that she wouldn't. There are some questions that are so difficult to answer. It is best to leave some things unexplained. Then the Curate came forward, rather humbly, and offered to put up a little prayer for patience and faith. He was shocked to see the change in the old worn face on the pillow; the end could not be far off, and the poor old soul was no more prepared for it than she had been months ago. The discipline of pain hadn't seemed to have answered in her case.

"I be past hearin' any prayers," she groaned, when the Curate would have knelt down by her side. "I've done nothing but pray day an' night, while I've laid here, an' the pain's worse instead of better."

Then the Curate had to tell her that the Heavens were not deaf as well as dumb, but the assurance fell on unheeding ears.

"I've a-prayed night an' day for years," she said in her querulous, complaining voice, "an' it's made no difference. P'r'aps the fault's in me, God knows! I've done my best; I couldn' do no more if I'd my time to go over again. I've brought up a family, and kep' out of the workus for nigh upon eighty years. I had a gal that was crippley an' not right in her mind, an' my husband was a bed-lier for years, an' I nussed 'em both, an' buried 'em without a penny from the parish. I couldn' do more."

No curate with a proper sense of duty could encourage the obstinate old woman in her ridiculous self righteousness. She had gone through a good deal, no doubt; few people reach four score without going through a good deal. They have their compensations, maybe, but this stiff-necked old creature had not had any compensations to speak of. The love of husband and children had been hers, but it had had its drawbacks. Her husband had been wont, when in health, to beat her black and blue, and to spend all her earnings; and her children had not been the comfort they might have been to her. Her life had been a failure from beginning to end. There was nothing she could remember in it to be grateful for. Looking back, it seemed to her that she had been more sinned against than sinning.

The Curate looking down from the height of his great happiness, at this poor soul groaning on her bed of pain, couldn't understand why he had been so supremely blessed, and she had suffered so much, and was still suffering. It was a mystery to himself; he couldn't pretend to understand it. He was only sure that God knew what was best for each, and had apportioned to each the discipline that best suited his case. To one the discipline of joy, to the other the discipline of pain and sorrow and loss. He couldn't explain this to Sarah Strong; she wouldn't have understood him if he had. He could only tell her that one day, no distant day, all these hard questions would be answered, and she would see that the Kind Hand that had brought her through so many trials had not laid upon her a single burden needlessly. It was not easy to tell her this when his own cup was overflowing; he felt in a blind, confused way, with a sense of shame and unworthiness, that the decrees of Providence were unequal; that to one was given the cup brimming over, to the other to wring out the bitter dregs.

Feeling all this he hadn't the heart to preach repentance and sorrow for sin; the poor old soul had had nothing but sorrow all her life, and if she had to live it over again, she would have done exactly the same; it didn't seem worth while to repent and be sorry, when if opportunity had served, she would have repeated the old mistakes and misdoing. He went down on his knees by the poor bed before he went away, and asked God to have mercy upon her—he couldn't think of anything better to ask—have mercy upon her, and upon him, and to give each the discipline He saw fit, to afflict, or to bless, according to

His unerring wisdom and love. He committed poor old Sarah Strong, and he committed himself, to the Love of God, which is over all, and around all, and makes no mistakes.

CHAPTER XI.

"A LITTLE RIFT WITHIN THE LUTE."

"It is not worth the keeping; let it go!"

LUCY COULCHER was a trifle more glum than usual when she got back to Cherry Garden. She was *distraite* and impatient, and out of sorts. It is not an uncommon malady, but it was new to Lucy. She was not exactly a pattern of all the virtues, but she ruled her spirit, or she strove to rule her spirit, which was much the same thing. She had an idea—it is not an entirely new idea—that the inner life is more to be considered than the outer, everyday life that is always coming into contact with the world, and chameleon-like, taking varying hues from its surroundings. The beautiful ideal inner life ever shaping itself within, could never be touched by these outside things. It had an independent existence; it was nourished by faith and hope and love, and the chisel that moulded it into shape was self-control.

Poor Lucy quite lost her self-control when she came back from that visit to Paradise. She was never quite herself after sitting an hour or two with Sarah Strong. The old woman insisted upon holding her hand all the time she sat beside the bed, and—Lucy would not have owned it for the world—it seemed to her, that by some occult process, hypnotic, mesmeric, or clairvoyant, that Sarah Strong's doubts and ill-humours were transferred to her during that long close hand-clasp. She always came away irritable and excited, with every nerve at tension and with her mind full of doubts and questionings.

She had come away in this abnormal state to-day. She had been asking herself all the way back, why the ways of Providence were so unequal? A good many people have asked the same question, and not found an answer ready to their hand.

Lucy had not found an answer when she got back to Cherry Garden.

She could not understand why some people should be so supremely blessed; should go through the world untouched by care or trial or suffering, while others should consume their lives away in pain. The pathos of Sarah Strong's life, while it moved her with infinite pity and compassion, aroused in her a smouldering sense of injustice which she could not stifle. What had Sarah Strong done that she should be so horribly poor, and have had such grievous trouble, and should suffer such excruciating pains? What had she done more than others? More than Nancy, for instance, who was singing downstairs, singing like a lark, whose life was brimming over with joy, who had lovers by the score—there was one going out of the gate as Lucy stood at the window. She could not understand why Nancy should have all the world at her feet, and be loved and petted and admired, while she and Augusta hadn't a lover between them, and never excited the least admiration, not the least little flickering flame in the hearts of the opposite sex. Lucy was not jealous; but she felt the injustice of Fate. With Sarah Strong, she felt that the ways of Providence were not equal.

"Mr. Asquith has only just left," Augusta said, coming into the room where Lucy was taking off her things. "He has been here all the afternoon. I believe Nancy means to accept him after all."

Lucy flushed in her sudden way. "She is only leading him on," she said scornfully. She had no patience with Nancy, and her tricks, and she could not keep the scorn and impatience out of her voice.

"I think it is more serious than that this time," Augusta said, stifling a sigh. "I only went in for a minute for a cup of tea, when I came back, and they were talking about a new carriage. Mr. Asquith was showing her a book with plates, and—and she has chosen a Victoria."

"You don't mean she has decided?" Lucy spoke in quite an awe-stricken voice; she was thinking of that look of happiness she had seen in Douglas Craik's face when he came into Sarah Strong's room. He couldn't keep his happiness out of his eyes. Any one could see it who looked at him, and could read the alphabet of love aright.

There is a look that one sees on the face of a girl in the early days of her first engagement, and on the face of a man sometimes, a man who is in love for the first time; having once seen it, one can never mistake it.

"She must have decided, or she wouldn't have chosen the colour," Augusta went on in her deliberate way. "Mr. Asquith preferred claret, dark claret, but Nancy would have blue."

"Then I suppose it's really settled."

It really looked as if it were settled.

Mr. Asquith was a constant visitor at Cherry Garden during the next week, and Nancy rode with him nearly every morning. There was nothing she enjoyed so much as riding, except dancing and playing tennis, each in its way. She had plenty of tennis at Stoke Edith, and dancing in the winter, but she had not had any riding since she left Cornwall, and then there had been only one old pony between all the family. The horse Mr. Asquith had got down for her from London was a great success; she had never had such a splendid mount in her life; and the habit that Lumby had lent her fitted her beautifully. It was quite the talk of Stoke Edith how well she looked on horseback.

Douglas Craik heard of those morning rides, there was no secret made of them, and smiled to himself when Nancy's engagement to Mr. Asquith was canvassed at the various tea tables, where it was a part of his duty to show himself. He could have thrown some light on that interesting subject if he would, but he was content to be silent. Why should he let these foolish reports move him? He had promised Nancy that he would trust her; that, whatever happened, he would trust her, and keep silence.

Miss Jayne was full of the report of Nancy's approaching marriage when the day came round for the curate to drink tea with her. There were so many duty teas and luncheons that he had to take with his parishioners, that he could not get through them all under a fortnight.

He had to keep a list of days, and parcel himself out. It was a form of parochial visitation—an agreeable form, and it saved his landlady a lot of trouble.

It was his day for visiting "The Bungalow," as Miss Jayne's myrtle-covered cottage was called. There were two Miss Jaynes, Catherine the elder, the sharp-tongued, kind-hearted gossip of Stoke Edith, and an invalid sister, Miss Grace, who was seldom seen off her sofa. They both clung to the traditions of their youth, and wore distended skirts and the hideous fashions of forty years ago. Miss Grace wore her own hair, which was thin and grey, in flat curls, fastened down with tortoise-shell combs on either side her kind face; but Catherine wore a front; a front of beautiful black glossy ringlets like those that Nature had endowed her with in her youth.

There was a painting of her over the

mantel-piece of the pretty, old-fashioned dining-room of the Bungalow, which was full of flowers and pictures and sunshine. It had been taken in her youth when the curls were her own, and the roses were blooming on her cheeks, and her eyes were bright. Her eyes were bright still, with a delightful old twinkle in them that no age could dim; but her cheeks had fallen in, they were ruddy, wholesome old cheeks, though their blooms had faded long ago, and her curls came ready-made from the *perruquier's* in the High Street. She had been a beauty once, in her day—she had had her day like the rest, she had not been cheated out of it—and she had still her bright eyes with the twinkle in them, and her jet black curls—they were hers still, though she paid Robinson in the High Street so much a quarter for keeping them in order.

Miss Catherine's black curls were nodding over the tea-cups when the Curate came in, and her lilac cap ribbons were bobbing about. She generally wore lilac or puce, or some kindred tint—she clung to the old colours as well as to the old gowns.

Something had happened that afternoon to excite her, and she was chirping over the tea-cups when Douglas Craik came in, and Miss Grace, propped up in an armchair at the other end of the long table with her silver trumpet to her ear—Miss Grace was a little deaf—was listening.

There was always a proper set tea at the Bungalow, none of the new-fashioned five o'clock standing-up affairs, but a sit-down tea at a well-spread board. The long dining table—Miss Catherine made tea in the dining-room—was dazzling with silver and china and flowers when the Curate stepped in out of the dusk of the verandah. The china was delightful old Derby china that had belonged to her mother, and the beautiful old silver had been in the family for generations, and the flowers had just come in from the garden, and the grapes and strawberries from the greenhouse. It was quite early for strawberries, but there was a lovely dish on the table, and cream and cakes and dainty biscuits, and home-made bread and butter. A dozen people might have been expected, instead of one small Curate.

"I am quite worn out," Miss Catherine said cheerfully—she was nodding her head and dropping in the lumps of sugar, and chirping like a cricket—"I have been out all the afternoon. I went for a drive with Martha Asquith, and she insisted on taking me over her brother's new house. She would not be satisfied until I had been over it from cellar to roof. She would not rest until I had been in the kitchen and seen the dresser that Nancy Coulcher had chosen. She has chosen everything in the house, he consulted her about everything——"

"I wish you wouldn't speak so fast, Catherine, I can't hear what you say!" grumbled Miss Grace at the other end of the table; "who did she say chose the kitchen dresser, Mr. Craik?"

She put the silver trumpet to her ear, and leaned forward, and Douglas Craik had to shout down it "Nancy Coulcher!" with the best grace he could.

"Nancy Coulcher!" the old lady repeated, nodding and smiling, and the Curate looked down at his plate.

"Martha had settled upon mahogany for the dining-room," Sister Catherine went on at her end of the table, not noticing the interruption, "good solid Spanish mahogany, there is nothing better, it lasts for generations." She glanced round as she spoke at the old-fashioned Spanish mahogany furniture of the room they were sitting in. It had already lasted three generations, and was as good as ever, "but Nancy would hear of nothing but oak, so he had to countermand the order."

"What is she saying, Mr. Craik? I don't hear a word," grumbled Miss Grace from her end of the table. She had put down her trumpet to drink her tea, and she had lost the thread of Catherine's discourse.

"Why wasn't he satisfied with a mahogany coffin; why did he want oak?"

Then the Curate had to explain.

"And the hangings are to be terra-cotta," Catherine continued unmoved from her end of the table, "pale terra-cotta. Nancy gave him the exact shade out of her colour box, and he carries it about with him."

"Terra-cotta linings to a coffin!" Miss Grace exclaimed, bringing down her trumpet with quite a rattle among the tea things. "I never heard of such a thing; the man must be going out of his mind; and why does he carry his coffin about with him? Someone ought to interfere."

Douglas Craik gave it up as quite hopeless; he couldn't explain any more, and Miss Catherine went on chirping among the tea-cups.

"The horses came in while we were there. I saw the groom taking them round, a chestnut and a roan. He bought the chestnut on purpose for her! he gave over a hundred guineas for it. It is a perfectly-trained lady's horse; it will not carry a gentleman; it is only fit for a lady. Nancy had been riding it all the afternoon, they had been out together. They go out every afternoon, now——"

"A roan and a chestnut for a funeral, I never heard such a thing! It was always black horses, coal black, in my time," Miss Grace was complaining from her end of the table. She had got hopelessly mixed with the kitchen dresser, and the mahogany coffin that was exchanged for an oak one, and nobody would explain.

The Curate had got up, he couldn't stand it any longer, he couldn't swallow another mouthful. The strawberries that had been gathered on purpose for him, that had been ripening for him for a week past, were untouched, and the cake that had been made for his especial benefit, his favourite cake, was uncut. He remembered suddenly that he had a visit to pay, and he got up and went away, and left the two old women to wrangle it out together.

Miss Catherine's black eyes saw that something was amiss, and she followed him out into the verandah to say good-bye.

"I thought you ought to know," she said humbly. "I thought you ought to know."

She went back into the shaded room, the silver and the china and the flowers dazzled her, or else there was a mist before her eyes that blurred them, and she turned away from the tea-table with a sigh, and took up some work she had laid aside before the Curate came in. It was a housewife she was making for him, a black, soft morocco housewife, and she was binding it with puce ribbon.

"I spoke very plainly," she was saying to herself, nodding her curls over the roll of puce ribbon in her lap, "but I thought it best. It is nothing more than the truth, and I'm sure he ought to know."

She was playing Providence as usual, it was her rôle, but sometimes she was in doubt, not often, whether it would not be better to let things take their course. She was not in doubt to-night; she was quite sure that she was doing her duty. She was sure that he ought to be warned.

"I wish you would come nearer, Catherine, and tell me about that funeral," whimpered Miss Grace from her sofa. "I couldn't catch who it was, and why he wanted his coffin to be changed."

CHAPTER XII.

IN THE RAIN.

Douglas Craik couldn't help telling Nancy what he had heard, the things that people were saying about her, what Miss Catherine had said about Ladylift, about the oak furniture and the terra-cotta hangings—and—and the kitchen dresser.

It was a very small bit of gossip to tell her; he felt it was quite mean and paltry to tell her, still she ought to know what people were saying.

She was so thoughtless, so candid, so open and unsuspecting, he told himself—she was all the sweet, ingenuous things that every woman is that a man is in love with—that she would lay herself open to—to unkind criticism, to harsh judgment, without a thought.

He met her one day when she was not expecting him, returning by the meadows from the Wilderness. She was not alone. Gilbert Earle, the mathematical master, was with her. He was not carrying her fiddle to-day, she had left that behind. It was raining a little, not much, not enough for a man to care about—a mere sprinkle, but he was carrying her umbrella. He couldn't hold it over her without getting under it himself. They were coming towards him across the meadow beneath that umbrella, and Earle was holding it rather forward, too forward for them to see him until he was close upon them.

He could hear their voices a long way off. There was no mistaking Nancy's voice, and her laugh. As Martha Asquith had ill-naturedly remarked, they could be heard "shouting" the other side of the road.

"Oh, hang it! there's that little prig of a

Curate," the schoolmaster said impatiently, when he saw Douglas a few yards off. "I hope you won't stop and speak to him, Nan——Miss Coulcher."

Nancy wouldn't have stopped to speak to him if she could have helped it. He stood right in her way, and he took off his hat in the rain, and he held out his little wet hand, and she was obliged to stop and shake hands with him, and tell him how her mother was. Mrs. Coulcher had been confined to her bed with influenza, and Lucy was nursing her. He had a message for Lucy from old Sarah Strong, who thought she was neglecting her, and he stayed to deliver the message. While he was delivering it the school bell rang and Gilbert Earle had to go away.

It was as much as he would do to reach the school before the bell stopped; he had come a long way out of his way with Nancy, and he had to set off at a run to be back in time. Nancy turned round to watch him running back over the wet springing grass. It did one good to see him run. A splendid athletic fellow, swinging along with great strides at the rate of ten miles an hour. His feet hardly seemed to touch the grass, and he took the hurdle that served for a gate, at a leap. He went over it like a bird, nothing stood in his way.

The Curate sighed as he watched him. He would have given the world for that splendid vitality, for that swinging step, for that robust, magnificent physique.

He would never be able to run like that, or to leap over a hurdle, if he lived till he were a hundred. He would always be a small, puny, frail creature, that could hardly bear the wind to blow upon him. This wetting—he was standing talking to Nancy in the rain, she was not offering him a bit of her umbrella—might cost him weeks of illness, might bring on another attack.

It did not seem much use caring and grieving, he had got to make the best of himself. Everybody had their limitations; he had not nearly so much to complain of as most people, Sarah Strong for instance.

Perhaps the thought of his own weakness arrested the words on his lips; the words he had come to say to Nancy. A flash of light, or rather a mist of rain, had revealed himself to himself as he stood there. His heart had been full of bitterness as he came through the meadow with the sound of their laughter in his ears, their glad, healthy laughter. The sight of that brawny giant flying across the grass was a reproof and a revelation.

What was he, he asked himself with a quick spasm of reproach, that this bright, beautiful creature should tie herself to him?

She was so strong and beautiful, quivering in every nerve with life and health; everything was before her, all the world, and the men were falling down at her feet. He could not think how it was that she had chosen him! He could not say any of the fine things he had come to say; the sight of her beauty, the touch of her hand, thrilled him with unutterable love and tenderness. What could he give her in exchange for this great gift she had given him?—only his life, which he was ready to spend in her service, to lay down at her feet, if need be, and let her trample over it. He was in her hands to use as she liked.

"You have something to say to me, Douglas," she said, looking at the little white-faced Curate standing there in the rain, when the big, stalwart fellow was out of sight; "you didn't come all this way to give me that message for Lucy."

He couldn't hide anything from her sharp eyes.

"No—o," he said slowly, reddening in a ridiculous way, "no, darling, there was something I wanted to say to you, to tell you," he said awkwardly, "to put you on your guard. People are so ready to put a wrong construction on things——"

"What have other people's constructions to do with me?" Nancy said, bridling up. "I suppose you have been listening to a lot of old women's gossip."

And then he told her what he had heard at the Bungalow, about her choice of the oak furniture for Mr. Asquith's new house, and the terra-cotta hangings, and the kitchen dresser. They were such paltry details, he was ashamed of himself for mentioning them; he was so sick of the whole thing, that he did not say anything about the horses, the chestnut she had ridden, coming back to the stable. It was like complaining of her, as if she had not the right to do as she liked. He had no acknowledged claim upon her. There was no link between them but the one she held in her own hand.

"You have been telling that woman of our engagement!" she said reddening with anger, and an impatient thrill in her voice that jarred upon him; "if you have told Catherine Jayne, it will be all over Stoke in an hour."

"I have not told anyone, darling," he said humbly. "I would give the world to be able to speak openly, to tell Miss Catherine and every one else that you have promised to marry me, Nancy!"

She turned upon him almost fiercely.

"If you are in such a hurry, if you can't wait, Douglas, we had better give it up. I would not have you tell people now for the world; what would be the use?—we can't be married for ages! I am sure mamma would not consent to a long engagement, to such a long engagement as ours would have to be. I—I thought you could trust me, Douglas——"

What could he say?

He would have given the world to have taken her in his arms—under the umbrella—and assured her that he would keep silence for ever, until she gave him permission to speak. He was yearning for love and sympathy; the tone of her voice jarred upon him, her sharp words cut him like a knife. He loved her with such absolute devotion, that he couldn't bear that there should be a momentary cloud between them.

She let him walk back beneath her umbrella, at least, she let him have all the drippings of it down the collar of his coat, and she suffered him to press her hand when he left her at the foot of the hill. She forgave him graciously for his ill-temper, and his cruel suspicions, as she called them, and she assured him that all that advice and assistance that she had given his Rector's brother in the choice of his furniture, and the colour of his hangings, meant nothing, that it was a mere act of charity.

"I couldn't help answering the poor man's questions, and telling him that Reckitt's blue wasn't good for the complexion," she said in her flippant way, as she wished him good-bye in the rain. "You are sure you don't mind my telling him he had better let the kitchen dresser alone? He wanted it painted an art colour, an æsthetic dresser, like those in Walter Crane's picture books; he was nearly out of his mind about it. He made Augusta quite ill, he used to bother her every day about it. It was like the Sphinx's riddle—to be, or not to be? It was out of pure charity I told him to let it alone. But perhaps you would rather he had had it painted, Douglas——"

She would not see things seriously. She would persist in making fun of things in her flippant, sprightly way.

He went away quite ashamed of his doubts, his vague jealousy melted quite away as he looked into the sweet bright face beside him.

Nancy's good temper had disappeared when she reached Cherry Garden. The tender love and trust that shone in Douglas Craik's steadfast eyes haunted her; she could not get them out of her mind.

Why would he take things so dreadfully in earnest? Why was he so horribly, so unreasonably jealous of her?

"He is dreadfully unreasonable and exacting," she told herself, as she came fuming up the hill; "he did not half recognize the sacrifices she was making for him." She was giving up a man with two thousand a year, and a position in the county, to marry a poor Curate who was dependent, or almost dependent, upon charity—she was thinking of those five-pound notes and the beef tea. He didn't consider the sacrifice she was making. She could marry anyone in Stoke—Gilbert Earle had almost asked her to marry him, he would have asked her if Douglas had not come up when he did; and then she fell a-thinking of the contrast between the two: the brawny giant striding over the grass in the lusty strength of his splendid manhood, and the frail little Curate shivering in the rain.

It was a cruel contrast.

When Nancy reached home rather draggletailed with walking through the wet grass, she found a letter from Mr. Asquith awaiting her. The Victoria had come down, and he wanted her to see it. He was not sure that it was the exact shade of blue. He would have it brought round the next day, and perhaps she would go out in it, she and Mrs. Coulcher. It should call for her at any time she would name. He had also sent her another book on beetles, one that he had edited, and he had written her name on the front page.

There was a hideous brown bug, on the frontispiece: he had called it by some long Latin name, and Nancy insisted on detecting a resemblance between it and the author. She flung the book aside with a shudder as she threw off her wet things. "What will you do about the Victoria?" Augusta asked. Augusta was helping her to take off her wet things.

"Oh, he can send it round if he likes; there's no harm in my seeing it. I needn't go out in it if he does send it round."

"No—o," Augusta said slowly, with a little catch in her voice, and her face drooping. She was pulling off Nancy's wet boots, and they were rather troublesome to unbutton, they were wet through with walking in the grass; "you need not go out in it unless—unless you have made up your mind. If you go out in it, you cannot very well draw back——"

Nancy laughed.

"How ridiculous and old-fashioned you are, Gus; as if anyone couldn't go out in a carriage without marrying the man it belonged to!"

"It isn't that," Augusta said in her odd jerky voice, with her drooping face growing pinker with the exertion of getting off those wet boots, "it's taken with the rest. You've helped him to decide about everything; the Victoria was got down for you; for a present to you. If you go out in it, it will be a tacit consent, you can't refuse him after that."

"Then I shan't go out in it," Nancy said shortly. "Mother's illness is quite a sufficient excuse. I can't think why he wanted to bother me about his things! I am sick of it all; no one knows what I've gone through about that kitchen dresser."

She was angry and out of sorts for the rest of the day. She forgot all about that message to Lucy. She was angry with Douglas for being unreasonable; she was angry with Catherine Jayne for talking about her, for spreading those reports; she was angry with Mr. Asquith for sending the Victoria. Why couldn't people let her alone? She only wanted to be happy—to be let alone—to live in the present. Why were people in such a hurry for her to get married? Why should she have to decide in a hurry?—there was plenty of time. She knew exactly what it would be if she were married—if she were married to Mr. Asquith. She would be shut up with him for the rest of her days in that great house, with the oak furniture, and the terra-cotta hangings—they would never wear out; he would buy such strong, substantial material that would never wear out, that would last for ever, and he would talk to her all day long about beetles and spiders, he would be always trying to teach her things, and she would get so sick of the sound of his voice, and the sight of his knitted gloves, and his cough, and his liver. The prospect was depressing. Not even the thought of the Victoria, and the chestnut in that loose box at Ladylift dispelled the gloom.

"What answer will you send Mr. Asquith, Nancy, about the carriage?" her mother asked her when she looked in for a minute to see if there was anything she could do for her. She hated nursing, and she couldn't bear sitting in a darkened room; she only looked in at the door of the sick room every day as a matter of form.

"Oh, I shall tell him you are in bed,

mamma; he can't expect me to go without you!"

"There is Miss Asquith; you could drive with her."

"I wouldn't drive with her for the world, the horrid old thing!"

"I shall be better in a few days, and up again—you had better sit down, Nancy, and write to Mr. Asquith; tell him I am looking forward to a drive in the Victoria the first day that I am allowed out."

It was her mother's message, not hers; it did not commit her in the least. She added a postcript to the letter, thanking him in her little exaggerated way for the lovely book he had sent her, that she was "longing to devour."

What could a lover desire more?

END OF VOL. I.

PRINTED BY
KELLY AND CO. LIMITED, 182, 183 AND 184, HIGH HOLBORN, W.C.,
AND KINGSTON-ON-THAMES.

www.ingramcontent.com/pod-product-compliance
Lightning Source LLC
Chambersburg PA
CBHW022008220426
43663CB00007B/1007